PERSONALIZED

PSALMS

The Psalms applied

to your world

Mike Holmes

Acknowledgements

A book is like a child. Before it is conceived, there have been genetic and environmental forces at work that bring the book to the moment of conception and then it grows in the womb of a mind. After a period of time it is given birth and becomes a baby, which is fed and nurtured until one day, it is fully grown and ready to be released to the world.

I thank all those, too many to mention, who have influenced my life in various ways as to help conceive this book and bring it to birth. There have also been many who encouraged me to continue feeding and nurturing it during its early development.

I specifically want to mention my wife, Cathy, who shared my enthusiasm and excitement as the book grew. My friends, Rob Jones and Paul Francis who have also been most positive all the way through the process.

Finally and most importantly, I want to acknowledge the work of the Holy Spirit, who, I believe, has been my inspiration.

Foreword

Many have a particular love for the Psalms. I guess mine developed as a boy when I heard the late Sir Lawrence Olivier reading the Psalms on my father's reel to reel tape player. His rich dramatic voice brought the Psalms alive for me and for a long time I tried to read them out aloud just like him!

The Psalms reflect the diverse human emotions we all have in an honest and sometimes very direct way. Over the years, as a preacher, I have pondered over how to approach some of the more aggressive language from the distant culture in which it was written. Some of the Psalms are what are called 'Messianic', that is, they are prophetically looking forward to the advent of the Christ. Most, if not all, of the Psalms can have a profound application and effect on our lives.

In this book, I have sought to make the Psalms very personal. Some of them are written as if they were a prayer or a direct conversation with God; others as if I was writing them. I would add, that, as an individual, I have not felt all the emotions and experiences found in the Psalms. Where the personal pronoun, 'I' is used in my book, this may or may not be me! These personalized psalms have also been written from the perspective of this side of the cross of Jesus Christ and the hindsight of the New Testament.

I need to strongly stress here, that this work is certainly not a translation or even a paraphrase of the Biblical Psalms. I am not a Hebrew scholar and I have not tried to interpret anything in the light of the original Hebrew text. These are, as the title suggests, personalized psalms based on the truths of the Psalms we love and know in our Bibles.

They are intended to be used as personal reflections to aid applying the Psalms to our lives in the 21st Century. They are my personalized psalms that I share with you. If they work for you, then I am pleased and would want to give God all the glory.

BOOK 1

Psalm 1

Happy am I when I do not take the advice of those opposed to God, or behave like them. I am happiest when I study, think about and practice the ways of God. When I do this, I am like a tree planted near a stream: I will bear the fruit that Jesus is looking for at the right time. I won't wither in the heat of troubles and difficulty. In fact, all that I do will prosper.

This is not the case for those who oppose God's ways. There will come a time when, like chaff, they will be blown away. There will be no place for them in God's kingdom. God looks out for those who love him, their future is eternal, but those who disregard God's ways will one day perish, with no hope of eternal life.

Psalm 2

Why do nations think they can conspire and plot against God's ways? Presidents, dictators and heads of state meet together to plan with no reference to the King of kings and the Lord of lords. In fact they actively rebel against God's ways and say, "Let's remove all restraints and the boundaries of the past. Let's get rid of the spiritual side of life."

But the all-powerful, almighty Lord of heaven and earth looks down and can only laugh at their pitiful rebellion. In fact he begins to speak to them in terrifying ways to let them know that he, the creator of all things, has installed his choice of king, which is Jesus, the anointed one, the Messiah, the Christ, on the throne in Jerusalem and he will reign over all the earth from there.

In fact, the Lord has spoken out a declaration to Jesus:

He said: "You are my Son; I am your Father. All you have to do now is ask, and I will give you all the nations as your inheritance, from pole to pole, it will all be yours. You will rule all these nations with a strong hand and all rebellion will be smashed to smithereens."

So be warned, those who lead nations. The wise thing to do is get God into your lives and nations. See him as the one you need to report to. Make peace with Jesus, consider him to be your Lord, otherwise you will end up destroyed. Don't put it off; you never know when his retribution might come.

If you really want to be happy, trust completely in the Lord.

Psalm 3

Lord, there are always those who would oppose what I am doing for you. Sometimes that is physical sometimes spiritual. They often try to cast doubt in my mind as to whether you will really be there when I need you.

But I want to acknowledge today that you are like a shield all around me. You make me look good. You help me walk tall. When I cry out to you, I find you answering me - how wonderful is that!

Knowing that you are looking after me helps me to get off to sleep at night. Fear is not on my agenda, even when it looks bad, because I know you care.

I am in a time when I need you to take special notice and come and deliver me from the opposition I am facing. Lord, will you render the opposition useless. Will you take away their bite?

I know you will answer me; you always turn up. O Lord, would you shower your undeserved favour on your people.

Psalm 4

O Lord, you do everything right, and I am asking you please to answer me. I am crying out to you to give me relief from the distress I feel. O Lord, please hear my cry, even when I know I don't deserve your help.

How long will people around me make me feel small? How long will they enjoy the gossip of others and chase after worthless things.

May they know that the Lord has his chosen people and he will hear them when they pray.

I must be careful when I get angry to not let it lead me into doing something bad. When I go to bed at night, I will think about my day; think about my attitude to things.

I will serve the Lord well whatever the cost and I will trust in him.

There are many people around who are asking if there is anyone who can help them. O Lord, will you shine through me, so that these people can see something of you in me?

There really isn't anything to beat knowing you; you fill me with deep joy, deeper than the superficial joy that I get when something really good happens.

I can always get off to sleep at night because I know that you, the Lord of the universe, have my best interest at heart.

Psalm 5

O Lord, please listen to my request for help, I really am at a low ebb. You are my God and my King, there isn't anyone else I would pray to. Here is the start of another day, will you hear me as I lay my requests before you, as I wait in expectation for you to answer.

You do not take any pleasure at all in the wicked things people do, in fact because you are so holy, people who do such things cannot even get close to you. Even arrogant people cannot be with you. You really do hate all the wrongdoings of people. Those who tell lies, those who are violent and those who are deceitful you particularly don't get on with.

I am so grateful to have found your mercy, your willingness to forgive my sin, so that I can enter right into your throne-room in heaven and in reverence bow before you. Lord, please lead me into doing the right things; there are some people around me who would want to lead me astray. Please make the path I should take very clear, for these people speak words that cannot be trusted, they are deceitful and only offer a path that leads to disaster. Lord, will you convict them of their sin. Will you make their schemes lead to their own downfall. Lord, they have really rebelled against you, will you leave them out in the cold for a while, so that they get the message.

When I come to you in my trouble, you make me glad again, in fact, I find myself singing for joy. Spread your protection over me like a security blanket so that I can rejoice always - I really do love you, you know.

There's one thing for sure, you place your favour on those who do the right things, who follow what you have said, who reflect your heart in what they do; in fact, they are surrounded by your favour - how wonderful is that!

Psalm 6

O Lord, I know I really deserve a dose of your anger, some form of discipline. But I appeal to you to have mercy, to hold back the punishment I truly deserve, because I am not feeling very strong right now. I feel rotten inside, stressed out. How long do I have to go on feeling like this? Lord, will you not come and sort things out - straighten out my life?

I know you love me with an unfailing love. I want to get back to praising you, but if this goes on for much longer, I won't be around to do that.

I am worn out, depressed. I can't seem to stop crying - I've gone through two boxes of tissues already. My eyes are bloodshot and puffy and I can't focus on anything.

Those who are against me better watch their step, for the Lord has heard my crying. He has heard me calling out for his help and I believe he is about to answer. All those against me will end up with egg on their face, defeated and will give up humiliated.

Psalm 7

Lord, you are my God, and I will come to you for refuge when I am in trouble. You are the one who will save me and deliver me from those who seek to destroy my life. Without you, I will get ripped to pieces, like a lion tearing its prey.

Lord, if I have any guilt on my hands, if I have done bad things to people who have simply tried to love me, if I have taken things from people without just cause, then I guess I deserve everything coming to me. However, I don't believe this is the case.

Lord, I ask that you rise up and deal with those that are against me, that justice may be done. My prayer is that everybody will eventually bow the knee to you, that they will let you rule over them, because your judgements are so right.

I trust you to judge me in the right way. I know you will put the right things I have done and my integrity into your scales. Everything you do is perfectly right. You are able to search the minds and hearts of people to find their true motives and their plans. Please bring an end to the terrible violence of evil men, and make those who are the good guys safe.

Actually, God is like a huge shield, protecting those who are good hearted.

God always judges people correctly, and consequently punishes people appropriately.

If God does not show mercy, watch out, he really does have some effective disciplinary procedures!

Those who are evil and plot evil deeds will eventually become disillusioned. They will fall into the hole they have dug for others; the trouble they have caused and their violent acts will rebound onto them.

I am so grateful to the Lord that I have experienced his perfect goodness. I feel like singing praise songs to him right now!

Psalm 8

O Lord, you're my Lord, and there is no-one in the whole world who gets even near how excellent you are. As I gaze into the universe at night, I think, "Wow, your glory is everywhere." Even through people who are as weak and vulnerable as children and babies you are able to silence those who oppose you, because you demonstrate your strength through them and in the end they give you praise because of what you have accomplished through them.

When I look up at the sky on a clear night and see the moon and the countless stars which you have put so meticulously into place - the vastness of it all makes me think about little old me, how it is that you can know me and care for me. How amazing that you have created me to be almost equal to the angels in heaven and have made available to me the very resources of heaven.

When you created people you made them to be the managers of all your creation - you put them in charge of everything. People are at the top of the food chain, all livestock, birds and fish are subject to us.

Like I said at the beginning, Lord, no-one in the whole world gets even near how excellent you are!

Psalm 9

O Lord, I want to praise you with everything I've got. I want to tell the whole world about the wonderful things you do. I'm so glad I know you, in fact, right now, I feel like bursting into a joyful song; I want to sing songs of praise to you, the highest God.

You turn back those who are against me; they don't get far and often just disappear. You are so good at fighting my corner - helping me get on with the good things I am trying to do - you are a great judge, meeting out what is right.

You even rebuke whole nations and get rid of the evil within them. Those that are evil within those nations will be blotted out of people's memories for ever. Disaster has overtaken them, their cities have been destroyed - even these cities will be remembered no more.

You O Lord, will reign forever, your throne is well established. When you judge the world it will be done in just the right way and you will continue to govern the people with perfect integrity. Already you are there for those who are oppressed and a strength to those who are going through times of trouble. Everyone who really knows you trusts you, because you never ever abandon those that are calling out to you.

Let's get together and sing praise songs to the Lord, the King of kings. Let's tell everybody what he has done. He is always interested in justice and where there is injustice, he will act.

Lord, I really feel persecuted right now. It's like being chased into a blind alley by a mugger. Please rescue me, get me out of there! I can't praise you like I want to at the moment in church; I want to rejoice again in the fact that I am saved.

Whole nations are going to the dogs because of their own folly. They are being brought down by their own deceptions.

The Lord is renowned for his justice. Bad people are so often caught in the very traps they have laid for others.

Everybody who forgets about God and just gets on with their own lives will eventually perish in the grave with no hope of eternal life. If they forget God, God will forget them, but God will remember the needy - he won't forget the prayers of those who have had a tough time.

O Lord, will you rise up and act. Don't let bad people get away with it. Many nations deserve your judgement. Would you make them see that even though they may have great power, they are only men and you are God? Whatever it takes!

Psalm 10

Lord, there are some things I don't understand sometimes. Like, why do you seem to keep your distance from me? Or, why do you seem to hide yourself from me when I really need you - when I am in times of trouble?

Bad people, in their arrogance and selfishness, trap weak people - they get caught up in scams. Bad people boast about the bad things they do; they are paly with other greedy people, but hate anything to do with God. Because of their pride, they don't bother trying to get God in their lives, there is no room for him in their busy schedules - they don't think they need him anyway. These bad people always seem to do well; as a result they are full of themselves. Your ways are not their ways. They just sneer at those who oppose them. They say, "Nothing fazes me; I'll always be happy and never have any trouble." Their mouths are full of bad words, lies and threats. When they speak they cause trouble, real trouble sometimes. They are the type of people that murder innocent people just for kicks - life is just a game. They lie in wait like a lion crouching in the undergrowth, waiting to pounce on the helpless and weak; they catch such people and then drag them off to their fate. Their victims stand little chance of survival. They are so conceited they say to themselves, "God has forgotten these pathetic people; he just covers his face and pretends not to see."

O God, it's time to act - to stop this evil - to help the helpless. How can these bad people have such a warped view of God? How can they think that he will not hold them to account one day? Lord, I know you see all the trouble and grief they have caused. You will help the victims of all this abuse. You help the most vulnerable in society. Lord, please disable the bad people, call them to account, let their deeds be exposed for what they truly are.

There is no doubt about it, the Lord is King for ever and ever! One day all his enemies will be defeated. My conviction is this: you hear the desires of those abused; you encourage them and you listen to their cries. You are the defender of the defenceless, the champion of the oppressed. Surely there is coming a day when terrorism of all kinds will be a thing of the past.

Psalm 11

It is in the Lord that I find my security, I don't need to listen to any advice about seeking it elsewhere. In fact, things are stacked against me so badly, my whole life seems to be falling apart, I have no alternative - it's the Lord or no-one!

The Lord is on his heavenly throne and from there he watches everything that goes on in the world. He sees those that are doing the right things, and he sees those who are evil and love violence. He really hates what the evil people do. In fact they are going to suffer the consequences of their action through God's judgement sooner or later.

The Lord's ways are perfect. He loves it when justice is done. You know, people who walk God's ways will one day see his face - now that is going to be awesome!

Psalm 12

Lord, where have all the good guys gone? They all seem to have vanished into thin air!

Everyone is speaking false and being false. They are two faced – 'bigging' people up without really meaning it. Lord, will you do something about this and the boasting that goes on? Some people think that they can talk their way out of, or into anything - they are so full of themselves they don't think they need anyone else - even you.

I hear you saying, Lord, that you are going to do something about the oppression of the weak and the groaning of those in need - that you are going to protect them from those who prey on them. Your words are pure, Lord, like the most purified gold in the world. I know you will keep me safe from oppressors. There are bad people who strut around like peacocks because they are treated with honour by some, even though they do some vile things.

Psalm 13

Lord, have you forgotten me? It certainly feels like it! How long have I got to wait before I get some help? How long have I got to wrestle with these thoughts in my head and the anguish in my heart? How long is it going to be before I get some light at the end of the tunnel?

Lord, you are my God, please can you look into my case and answer my requests. This tunnel is so dark and I feel like death warmed up. I can hear those against me soon whispering, "We've got him!" They are going to really feel smug.

However, I will continue to trust in your unfailing love and my heart will be full of joy because I am saved. Yes, I will sing some songs to you, Lord, because, come to think of it, you really have been so good to me.

Psalm 14

How foolish to think that God does not exist. When people think like that, God's boundaries disappear and corruption, immorality and bad ways creep in.

God is looking down onto the earth to see if there are any people who are still seeking after him, who understand him. It seems like everyone has turned away from God, everyone has become corrupt and there is not even one that does good.

Will the ungodly never learn? They consume God's people like a hungry man eats breakfast, and they never pray. However, they are full of fear, knowing deep down that God is with his people. They try to fleece even the poor, but God will come to their rescue.

I'm looking forward to the time when God's people will be totally at peace, when all is well with them - that will be a day of great rejoicing!

Psalm 15

Who can live constantly in God's presence? Anyone who does nothing wrong, who always does what is right, who always speaks the truth, who never has a bad word to say about anyone, who lives at peace with those around him and never gossips, who hates the bad things some do, who gives honour to those who love God, who keeps their word even when it hurts to do so, who are happy to lend money to people without demanding interest and who do not accept bribes.

The person who does these things will never be evicted from God's presence, will always be a solid person.

Psalm 16

Lord, please keep me safe from harm - I really do see you as the one to come to when I am in trouble. You are my Lord and you are my everything.

When I think of all the wonderful Christians in the world, it makes me feel good. Eventually those who chase after false gods, whatever they may be, will become full of sorrow. I have made up my mind, I will never have anything in my life that is more important than God.

Lord, you provide everything I need and I feel really secure in you. It feels like you have favoured me, and when I think of the future you have got lined up - I am so excited!

You are so worthy of praise, my Lord, you are the one who guides me, even at night you pour wisdom into my life. You are always in the forefront of what I do, you are always right there beside me and I know that nothing need faze me.

Because of this I feel so happy inside, and there is a song always on my lips. Even when I die, my body will rest in peace waiting for the glorious day of the resurrection, because you have shown me the path that leads to eternal life. When I am finally in your presence forever, what joy and pleasure I will know.

Psalm 17

Lord, can you hear me? Please listen to my cry for help, please lend an ear to my prayers - they do come from a genuine heart. I want you to vindicate me; to see what is right and wrong here. You can shine a bright light into my heart and examine it closely, you can put me to the test, but you will find nothing wrong. I have made a vow with myself that I will not let my tongue speak anything bad. I have never been violent to anybody. I have endeavoured to keep my feet walking the path you would want for me; I have never slipped up.

Lord, I am calling to you; I know you will answer; I need you to lend me your ear - to hear my prayer. Will you show the wonder of your incredible love? You always save those who have you at the centre of their lives from their enemies. It is wonderful to know that I am the apple of your eye, protected in the shadow of your wings from those who would do me harm. They seem intent on ending my life - they show no mercy and they speak out of their arrogance. They have tracked me down and now surround me. In their eyes I see a determination to finish me off. They remind me of a hungry lion crouching in the undergrowth ready to pounce.

Lord, I need you to rise up, confront them and defeat them. I need rescuing by your mighty sword from them.

You feed those who you love, their children have plenty and there is an inheritance to pass on. I know I will one day see your face. When I awake from death I will be fully satisfied because I will be like you.

Psalm 18

Lord, I want you to know that I love you. You are my strength, my rock, my castle, my deliverer, my refuge, my shield, my salvation, my stronghold. I called out to you and you saved me from those who were against me. You really are worthy of praise.

I was close to death; I could feel myself being swept towards the grave. It was like ropes were dragging me towards an early grave; I was face to face with death. In the depths of despair I called out to the Lord, I cried for help and he heard me; my cry came directly into his ears. What happened next was awesome: there was an earthquake, the very foundations of the mountains were shaken - everything was trembling because God was angry. There was fire and smoke coming from heaven as God parted it and descended on dark clouds. He then climbed onto the back of some angels and flew like the wind under the cover of darkness. And then, due to the brilliance of his presence, clouds clashed, causing hailstones and bolts of lightning. The Lord was thundering from heaven and his voice could be heard everywhere. He shot arrows of lightening from his bow and scattered those who were against me. Even the deep crevices of the sea and the foundations of the earth were exposed at the blast of God's rebuke.

He reached down from the lofty heights of heaven and took hold of my hand and drew me out of the deep water I was in. He rescued me from everyone and everything that was against me and too strong for me. They thought they would bring me down, but the Lord himself was my support. He brought me out of the dark tunnel into open space; he rescued me because I was a delight to him.

God has been good to me because I have endeavoured to always do the right thing. I have walked on the road God has marked out without deviating. The things that God has said I have been obedient to; there are no blots on my copy book, which is why God has been so good to me.

You are seen to be faithful, blameless and pure to those who try to be like you. Crooks, however, will find how shrewd you are.

You are happy to rescue the humble, but you don't have time for the proud.

You are the one who keeps the fire in my heart alight and you turn the light on when my mood is getting dark. With your help I can face a whole army of opposition; I can get over the highest obstacle.

Lord, I have to say, your ways are just perfect; and no-one can pick the smallest hole in what you say. You are like a shield to everybody who looks to you for protection. There certainly is no other God except you. There is no other I would base my life on except you. You are the one who gives me strength when I need it and guides my feet onto just the right paths. In fact, I feel like my feet will never slip from the upward path you have placed me on. When it comes to the battles I find myself in, well, now I realise that you have been training me for this for a long time; the spiritual muscles I have developed help me deliver hefty blows on those things which come against me. In fact, victory is assured because you are right there with me in the battle; you stoop down from heaven and make me look good. You make what was a tight-rope walk into a wide path - I don't have any worries of falling over.

What a great day it was when I chased those things that were hounding me, I caught up with them and dealt with them once and for all. Now I am completely free of them - they will never come back - they have been destroyed forever beneath the feet of Jesus on the cross. I will not forget that it was you who gave me the strength to win; it was you who made the demons come under subjection; it was you who made them flee from me and be destroyed. How ironic that they should cry to you for mercy, but you were having none of it, you didn't even bother to answer them. They have become like dust blowing in the wind, like mud on a bridle-path.

Not just demons - you have delivered me from people who have been against me. You have given me a high position and people I do not even know are under my authority. When they hear one of my orders, they have to obey. Even those who are not your people have to toe the line. They find no comfort in their own patterns of thinking anymore.

I feel a song of praise coming on! I want to declare the obvious: The Lord is alive! He should be praised and honoured. He is my Saviour. Lord, you did the impossible, you lifted me out of danger, out of certain death. Therefore, I will praise you wherever I go, and sing praise songs to you. He gives great victories and unfailing kindness to his people.

Psalm 19

Just take a look at the stars, the clouds, the blue sky, a sunrise or sunset, when you look up whether it be night or day, everything just shouts out, "God made all this - his glory is all over it - how wonderful, great, awesome God is - how limitless his knowledge."

It doesn't matter where you go on this planet, it doesn't matter what language you talk in - everywhere the awesomeness of the sky and the universe speak volumes.

God placed the sun in just the right place in the universe; what an impressive sight it is when it emerges over the horizon - a champion of stars. It circuits from one end of the sky to the other so that nothing escapes its heat.

God's rules are perfect and when I obey I get more out of life. These rules can be trusted, and when obeyed make me wise. These rules are just the right thing to do, and when obeyed I have joy in my heart. These rules are brilliant, and when obeyed my outlook is brighter. These rules help me revere God in a pure way, which will last for ever. These rules are solid and totally right; they are more precious than the purest gold and sweeter than honey taken straight from the comb. These rules warn me against certain actions and when I obey them I will reap great rewards.

However, these rules are difficult to keep, so please forgive me, even for those things I don't realise I have done wrong. O Lord, keep me from wilfully going astray - I don't want to be in a situation where I am chained like a slave to my wrongdoings - where they get the better of me all the time. I want to live a blameless life, never doing anything of consequence wrong.

O Lord, as I ponder these things and make declarations before you, I trust they will please you. I want to please you, because you are my everything - my foundation, the one who has bought me with a great price.

Psalm 20

May the Lord come to your rescue when you need him; when you use his name against the devil and his demons, may you find yourself shielded by angels. May the Lord send help straight from his throne-room - a legion of angels to support you. May he remember all the sacrifices you have made for him and the worship that has ascended to him from your heart.

May he give you the very thing you desire and may all the plans you are making be successful. We will all rejoice with you when you get the victory you seek and we will praise God together. May the Lord give you the things you are asking him for.

As for me, I know the Lord has given me victory; he has answered me from his throne-room using his almighty power. Some trust in the strength of their bank balance, others in their status in society, but we trust in the Lord to whom all things belong and the amazing thing is - he is our God – talk about name-dropping! Those who trust in other things will eventually fall off their high horses, whereas we will keep moving onwards and upwards, standing firm.

O Lord, in a nutshell, save me and answer when I call!

Psalm 21

O Lord, I am so pleased I have your strength behind me. When I see the victories I have because of you I am bouncing with joy. You have given me what I asked for, the very thing that was on my heart.

You have shown me your great favour, I feel like I have a crown of gold on my head - so honoured am I. I asked for eternal life and you have given it to me; life that will never end.

Through these victories, you have made me look good; I certainly feel like a king. This favour is straight from heaven and I feel you are so close - O what joy I have. I trust in you, Lord. I know that because you love me with an unfailing love, I will never be fazed.

I wouldn't like to be in the shoes of your enemies when you get hold of them. They will be destroyed in a fiery furnace - swallowed up by the flames and consumed. Even their descendants will disappear and their wealth will be no more. They may try to plot evil deeds - wicked schemes - but they will never succeed. Eventually they will be chased away.

O Lord, I want you to be so lifted up and honoured because of your great strength. I will sing praise to you - you can count on that.

Psalm 22

Those words of Jesus on the cross come to me today, "My God, my God, why have you forsaken me?" You seem far from saving me, far from the groans of my heart. I am crying out to you night and day, but I hear no answer. I remind myself that you are King of kings, that you are the one who is continually praised by your people. Past generations have put their trust in you and you delivered them; they cried out to you and you saved them; they trusted in you and were not disappointed. I feel so wretched; I feel like a worm rather than a human being. It feels like everybody is poking fun at me, despising me, insulting me. I can see them shaking their heads and saying things like, "He trusts in the Lord, well, let the Lord rescue him. He loves the Lord, well, let the Lord deliver him." Come to think about it, this is just what Jesus went through on the cross.

Let's state a couple of facts: it was you who brought me to birth and I am privileged to have been brought up to put my faith in you as my God from the delivery room. So, Lord, do not hide from me now, there is trouble brewing and there is no one else to help.

The devil and his demons are dancing around me; like roaring lions tearing at their prey, they open their mouths menacingly in front of me. It is as if my whole life is being poured out like water onto the ground. Everything is out of joint in my life. My emotions are wrecked, they have no substance anymore. My strength is crumbling to pieces, my mouth is dry, I am close to death. Dogs sense the imminence of my death and are surrounding me. I am being crucified. I am but skin and bones and people stare at me. They are even taking my few remaining clothes and gambling for them.

Lord, please be close to me at this time. You are my strength and I need you to help me. I need you to send me a rescue package, there are weapons, powerful dogs, lions and wild bulls to deal with.

I will proclaim your name and praise you in church. Come on, you who love God, praise him with me. You who have been counted in as the people of God - honour him, bow down to him. Because he has not turned away from my suffering; he has not turned a blind eye to my cry for help.

You provide such a great theme for praise. The vows I have made will be fulfilled. Those who seek after you, even the poor and hungry, will be satisfied and praise you.

One day, the whole world will turn to the Lord, people from every nation will bow down before him, because the world belongs to him anyway and he is the ultimate ruler. Every rich person, all those who are crushed, broken, oppressed and those who are unable to keep themselves alive due to their appalling conditions will end up worshipping the Lord. This will be a generation of God's people who will serve him, and to those yet to be born - they will proclaim God's goodness.

Psalm 23

The Lord is my personal guide. He is just like a shepherd looking after his sheep. When I am following him I will never have any lack in my life. He takes me to the places where I can feed my soul and rest; where I can quench my spiritual thirst; where I can be restored. He guides me along the right paths in life. Yes there are going to be difficult paths where dark shadows prevail, but I have nothing to fear because the good Shepherd is right there with me and I will be comforted with the knowledge that he can protect me and bring me out of any danger.

Lord, you are the one who has provided a feast of good things for me, despite my enemies advances. I feel your favour, your blessing, all over me; I feel like a glass that is overflowing. Surely your goodness and love are going to follow after me for the rest of my life and one day I will find myself in the midst of your presence for the rest of eternity.

Psalm 24

Every part of planet Earth belongs to the Lord. He designed it and brought it into existence and so everything in it and on it, and everything that lives, are his. Now, out of all the people on the earth, who are the ones who can approach God and stand before him? It has to be those whose lives are clean and whose motives are pure; people who put God first in their lives and do not put their faith in anything or anyone else. They will receive favour from the Lord; they will be shown to be right. May there be such a generation of people who seek after God, who long for his face to shine upon them. May I be one of them.

And so I say to the doors of my heart, those doors that have not been open for a long time, "Swing wide - so that the glorious king may enter." You may ask, "Who is this glorious king?" Well, let me tell you; he is the Lord who is so strong and mighty; he is the Lord who always wins. And so I say to the doors of my heart, those doors whose hinges have become rusty - "Swing wide - so that your glorious king may enter." You ask, "Who is this glorious king?" Let me tell you, he is the all-powerful, almighty Lord, the captain of a countless multitude of angels - that is who he is!

Psalm 25

I bare my soul only to you, Lord, because you are the only one who I can completely trust. So, don't let me down, Lord, don't let those who are against me win. Everyone who puts their hope in you will find things working out for their good. Those who go against you, will end up with red faces.

Therefore, reveal more of your ways to me, Lord, teach me how to walk along your paths. Be my guide, be my teacher, so that your truth may be the foundation of my life. You are my God, my Saviour, and I will put my trust in you twenty four hours a day.

Lord, your incredibly great love and forgiveness for me has always been there, even when I was young and rebellious in my ways, how amazing is that! You are so good, Lord, please keep that love and forgiveness flowing towards me.

Because you are so good and do everything right, you are happy to help the wayward find the right path. You guide those who realise they can't do it on their own; you teach them your ways which are infused with love and faithfulness.

Lord, I have made some big mistakes, please forgive me.

I do respect your authority over me and want to listen to you and find out what you want me to do. I know that if I find the purpose you have for me, I will be prosperous and those that come after me will benefit from what has happened.

You are keen to let me in on your plans and make promises. I really need to focus on you, because you are the one that will get me out of any traps I fall into.

Lord, turn your face towards me and shower me with your grace, because I feel pretty lonely right now and things are weighing me down. It seems like there is trouble around every corner and I need you to deliver me. So, please take a look at what is happening to me and please forgive the part I have played. It seems like those who don't like me are multiplying and some of them are so cruel. I need you to guard me, rescue me, stand up for me; you are my refuge.

I am trying to be honest and do the right thing, but my real hope is in you.

Please get me out of all my troubles!

Psalm 26

I haven't lived a bad life, please stick up for me Lord. I have always trusted you - you can see that for yourself by just looking into my heart and reading my mind. I am constantly aware of your love and endeavour to make my life's journey be based on your words which are always true. I don't have time for people who manipulate and are two faced. I feel uncomfortable around people who wilfully do wrong things - I don't want anything to do with them. I find cleansing when I come to Jesus, it feels good and I can't help but let out some praise and let other people know how great you are.

I love being close to you, soaking in your glory.

There are some who are out to get me, there are temptations at every corner, but I intend to live clean. I need your help, your deliverance and at times your mercy and grace.

I feel like my feet are on solid ground. I can't wait to get to church and worship you with everybody else.

Psalm 27

The Lord lights up my life, helps me see the way and has certainly saved me from destruction, therefore I have absolutely nothing to be afraid of. The Lord is like a castle for my life to be safe in, so why should I be afraid of anyone? The very people who are out to get me, will themselves stumble and fall. I am so confident in the Lord, that even if a whole battalion should come against me, or a full-scale war break out against me, I will not be afraid.

There is really only one thing I would ask of the Lord and just the one thing I would seek and that is to live in God's presence every single day of my life. There is nothing better than being able to focus on how beautiful God really is and to spend some quality time with him. When troubles come, I know I am safe because he is with me; his very presence is all around me, I feel like I am looking down on the problem from a secure place. He keeps my head above the water and so I will praise him out of sheer joy with music and song.

Lord, I am speaking with you, please listen. I know I don't deserve it, but please answer me. My heart is speaking to me and saying, "Spend some time with God." So, that is what I will do. As I do that, please don't hide or turn away from me - I can understand that you might want to, given my behaviour, but you are the one who helps me. I couldn't bear it if you rejected me or left me. What am I saying? I know that even if my own father or mother were to leave me, you Lord would never do that. Please teach me how to live, to walk straight in life - there are many things out there that could put me off my stride. Do not lead me into temptation, deliver me from evil.

I am very confident that I will see God's goodness all around me. So, I am going to be strong and wait for God to turn up.

Psalm 28

There is no one else but you that I am calling on, Lord, so please listen. If I don't hear you I will feel so empty. Hear me, hear my cry for help. Look, I am lifting up my hands to heaven!

I don't want to succumb to peer pressure and do the wrong things others are doing. I don't want to be like those who are two faced - saying one thing but harbouring another in their hearts. They will eventually reap what they sow, get what they deserve - payback time is coming - unless they turn their eyes to the cross and mend their ways.

Praise God, because he hasn't given me what I deserve. The Lord has become my source of strength; he is like a shield for my protection; he is my helper and I trust him wholeheartedly.

There it goes again, that desire to break out in song and praise God out of sheer joy.

Oh God, you are the strength of all those who put their trust in you - you are certainly like a castle for me, where I find safety. I know you are like this for all those who belong to you, and I ask for your blessing on them and that you will be like a shepherd to them, caring, protecting and comforting them for all time.

Psalm 29

Let everything within me acknowledge God's incredible character and power. Let me acknowledge everything about God that is worthy of his name. Let me worship him as I reflect on how awesome he really is.

The very voice of God is worth contemplating. It thunders like a waterfall, or the rapids of a river, or the breakers on the rocks of the shore; it is so powerful, even majestic. It is able to make firewood of the strongest of trees. It can cause the ground to shake, lightening to flash, hurricanes to blow. God, you are amazing. Whatever catastrophe is going on in my life - you are still reigning as my king and will do forever. You will always give me strength to carry on and fill me with peace beyond my understanding.

Psalm 30

I will lift you up, Lord, because you lifted me up - up out of the depths of despair - before people started to talk. I called out to you for help, and you brought healing to my mind. You brought me out of the darkness of the tunnel and spared me from taking my own life.

It's time to praise God; to sing about him. His anger is only momentary, but his favour lasts a whole lifetime. I may find myself crying in the night, but when he is around, I will be full of joy by the morning.

Sometimes I feel so secure in you and I think nothing will ever faze me. When your favour is all over me, I feel totally safe. But when you seem to hide your face from me, I get confused. I remember calling for help, crying out for mercy; using arguments like, "What is the point in letting me go under?" Or, "What is the point in letting me die, because I won't be able to praise you when I am but dust, I won't be able to tell others about how faithful you are then?" So, will you hear my cry for help now? Please help me.

Wow, thank you. You have turned things totally around. My crying has been turned into dancing, my mourning into joy. It's happening again - that overwhelming desire to sing to you - I can't keep silent. O Lord my God, I just want to give you thanks for ever and ever.

Psalm 31

Lord, you are like an embassy building in which I have found refuge as one of your citizens, so don't let me be caught by those out to embarrass me. I need rescuing quickly so listen to my plea for you to be the rock I can firmly stand on and the castle I can run into and be safe. Since you are these things, lead and guide me towards them. There is a minefield out there that I need you to get me through. I place my very life into your hands - I ask you to pay the price for my liberty.

How pointless to put your trust in anything, or anyone other than the Lord. I am full of joy when I think of your love for me. You saw the pickle I was in and the despair it brought me and you guided my feet along a path that has brought me into a place with a pleasant view.

Go gentle with me Lord, I feel pretty stressed, washed out, weak. My life seems to be one long string of disasters, year after year. I can't take much more; I just want to curl up in a ball. People are talking about me behind my back, even my closest friends don't want anything to do with me anymore. I feel so rejected, like a broken, cheap ornament that is simply thrown away. People are saying untrue things about me; they really want to see the back of me.

But I still trust you, Lord. I say to myself, "You are my God." Your timing is perfect. You will deliver me from my troubles and from those who want to get rid of me.

May your glorious favour and unfailing love come to my rescue. Do not let me suffer embarrassment; I am crying out to you - let the wayward be embarrassed and be silenced. Let their lies be silenced, for they are full of pride and contempt, speaking with much arrogance against those who follow you.

There are vast quantities of your goodness that you have stored up for me and you are going to shower me with it so that all can see. Your very presence shelters me from some of the evil schemes of people; you keep me safe from their accusing tongues.

I praise you, Lord, because you have showed me your wonderful love when I was oppressed on every side. At the time I thought, 'Can God see me?' Yet you heard my cry for help, you answered.

I love you Lord. You preserve my life and this knowledge brings me inner strength and fills me with hope.

Psalm 32

How great it feels when what we have done wrong is forgiven by God and he decides not to see it any more, keep no record of it. It makes me feel clean on the inside.

When I carried the burden of my wrongs, it was as if they became like acid inside me, eating me up; they were heavy and my very strength sapped away like when it is very hot.

It was then that I confessed my wrongs to you, Lord, I couldn't cover my sin from you any longer - only you can cover sin. As soon as I got it off my chest and spoke it out to you all the guilt just melted away and I knew I was forgiven. How cool is that! Everybody should do it - just talk to God because he is there. Whatever is going on, God can sort it out. I am going to make God the place I go to when I need to hide from the storms of trouble that sometimes surround me and listen to him singing a song of comfort and encouragement to me.

Now I am in the right place again, I can benefit from God's instruction and teaching; his advice and protection. I have been so stubborn and rebellious and yet I have always, deep down, trusted God and his love has always been there through thick and thin.

So, I am singing again on the inside and on the outside, as I contemplate how clean I now am through his forgiveness and grace.

Psalm 33

I have every reason to sing joyful songs to the Lord and it is right that I do because of his grace. I will join in with those who are good at leading worship with various instruments. I will even make up new songs that come from my joyful heart.

When God speaks, he is always right and everything is true. He is so faithful to me. When I look around, I see his love demonstrated in so many ways. He loves things to be right and fair for the people he has made.

It was just his spoken word that brought the universe into existence with all those countless stars. Then there were all the countless litres of water he gathered and put into place. When I think of such things I am reminded of God's greatness and I need to treat him with the utmost respect. He just spoke and all creation came into being!

God is a global God, he is able to intervene in the plans of nations and people groups. God has got a plan that stretches into eternity and nothing can thwart it. God has purposed in his heart good things for me.

When a nation acknowledges God as its Lord, that nation is blessed. God is able to see everybody on the earth, all the billions of people and everything they do. Even a strong king is not really safe despite the size of his army. What they really need is God on their side, and he will be if they acknowledge him, respect him and put their hope in him.

So, when it comes to me, I need to put my hope in the Lord, realising that he is there to help and protect. Then, whatever is happening, I can rejoice because my trust is in him. O Lord, as I put my hope in you, may your unfailing love envelop me.

Psalm 34

What a great way to live – always with God in mind, always 'bigging' him up. I will show how good it is to know God and hope that others, particularly those with problems, will find the joy of knowing him too.

Let's all raise God's profile and make his name great. I needed some answers and God showed up; my fear disappeared.

When I spend time with him, I feel radiant and my face shows it.

There are countless examples of the poor asking God for help and finding themselves delivered from their problems.

It's remarkable to realise that angels surround me; angels are working invisibly for me.

Oh, how good God is; I am so blessed that I have found him. I know that I will lack nothing, no good thing. Anyone out there who is prepared to listen, let me help you see how great God is.

The more I tame my tongue to speak only good and truthful things, the more life I will enjoy.

I need to walk in the opposite direction to evil along the path of good. I need to be an active peacemaker.

God's eyes follow me as I do the right things and he hears me the moment I ask for help. On the other hand, God hates evil and eventually those that do evil things will receive their just desserts.

When I am doing the right things, God hears me when I need his help and gives me a 'get out of jail free' card.

God is really close when my heart is broken and he stoops down to raise me up.

Even when I am doing all the right things, I am not exempt from trouble, but I know that God will get me out of every hole. Actually he is my protector.

The evil deeds of bad people will eventually be their downfall, and those opposed to people trying to do the right thing will not get a 'get out of jail free' card.

When I am serving God, he will rescue me when I am in a pickle. When I run to God, he won't condemn me for the mess I made.

Psalm 35

Lord, I am looking for some justice. As I am fighting for your cause, there are those who fight back. They are antagonistic towards me, because I bear your name. So, I am looking for some help here, some weapons that will win the day. I know you are my Saviour.

It is not my place to bring people to justice, only yours. I am confident that you will deal with people according to their deeds in the most perfect way. So I leave that to you. However, as I am pursuing your kingdom, I need some victories now. So, will you thwart the schemes and manipulative ways of those against me. Show them up for who they are, so they slip up on their own dark paths, get entangled in their own net and fall into the pit they had dug for me.

When I am vindicated and those against me are now for me, then I will be so relieved and full of joy. I will burst into praise because you have saved me, because you love justice, because you hate oppression.

I find it difficult to cope sometimes with getting back evil for the good I have done. The same people that I sacrificially helped, prayed and fasted for as I would for members of my own family, have turned against me.

They now laugh at my misfortune. They slander and gossip about me. They even laugh in my face and try to intimidate me.

So, Lord, how long will you allow this to go on? Please, rescue me from this onslaught. I am looking forward to sharing my testimony of your intervention to the congregation.

So, again, please don't let these people, who have no rhyme or reason for their actions, get away with it. They are stirring up trouble and making up untrue stories against peace loving people.

They claim to have witnessed things that I have not done. But Lord, you know the truth, you see all things. So, please don't stand at a distance here. Instead, come and do something about it. Vindicate me. Stop their gloating; their thinking that they have finally destroyed me.

In fact, could you turn the tables on them, so they will be ashamed, confused and disgraced.

I know there are others who want to see me vindicated. I am looking forward to the time when they will be celebrating with me and praising you for your delight in my well-being. And my tongue will also speak out how good you are and praise you all day long.

Psalm 36

I have had a revelation concerning bad people. They simply have no fear of God filtering their deeds. They actually see their bad behaviour as commendable, carrying forth evil acts like trophies of honour. Their language is foul; their words are full of venom and not to be trusted. The capacity to show some wisdom and goodness has long gone. Even when they are resting they are hatching new plans to do harm and they hug the road of sinfulness without deviation.

Let me have a revelation about you, O Lord:

Your love knows no bounds, your faithfulness reaches far beyond what I can see. All the right things you do pile up like mountains and all the just things you do go deep into the cultures of the world. You care about people and you care about animals.

No-one can put a price-tag on your love – it keeps on flowing like an everlasting stream. It doesn't matter if someone is born into royalty or poverty, they can both find refuge from the storms of life in you. They can both have a banquet of abundant life and both drink deeply from God's fountain of delights.

For it is in God my life erupts like a volcano and through his light all my darkness disappears.

O Lord, may your love and blessing be ever with me. Guard me against pride and deliver me from the temptations that surround me. For I see how some lie fallen and unable to get back up.

Psalm 37

I will not concern myself unduly over bad people and certainly won't be envious of those who do wrong things and seem to get away with it, because eventually they will get their just desserts.

No, I will trust in the Lord and do good things so that, on balance, I will live more safely.

God has promised that when I play my part in the relationship I have with him, he will give me the very things I desire. When I actively commit myself to walking the path he has set out for me and trust him along the way, then he promises to make his blessing on my life very clear and any vindication obvious.

So it is so good for me to periodically take opportunity to get away from it all and just rest in God's presence, waiting there until I hear him. This helps me not to get upset when things go wrong due to the actions of others. It is so important to not get angry and start looking for ways to get even, because this will just lead to wrong doing on my part.

I need to remember that those who do bad things will receive justice eventually and those who put their hope in the Lord will receive eternal life.

Compared to eternity, the timeframe is relatively minute before wickedness will be a thing of the past. When that time comes, it is the meek that will enjoy peace and prosperity.

The bad people hatch plots against the good people, snarling like wolves at times, but God looks into the future and knows the day of judgement approaches.

The bad people devise plans, even wars, to obtain power and feather their own nests – bringing down anyone who gets in their way. However, their plans will backfire eventually and they will be overthrown.

It is infinitely better to be one of the good people with little than one of the bad people with much. Ill-gotten power will be broken, but God will support those who do things the right way. In fact, those who have accepted Christ as their Saviour will find themselves living under the Lord's care every day and their future will be eternal. In times of trouble they will be upheld and in the lean times they will receive God's provision.

On the other hand, those who reject Christ will perish. Those who are in rebellion to God will be like flowers in the field consumed by livestock or burnt. Such people borrow but they never repay, whilst the good people love to give generously. God's grace leads to eternal life, but God's judgement leads to eternal death.

When the Lord is my passion, he makes me walk through life with firm steps and even when on occasions I stumble, I don't fall over because he reaches out his hand and grabs me like a loving father.

I am not as young as I used to be, I have experienced a fair bit of life, but I have always found God in the midst of it all and have never been without food on the table. I have found God's generosity rubbing off on me and my children have been such a blessing.

My advice is for us all to turn from our ways to God's ways, for in him there is absolute security. The Lord is faithful and loving to those who are faithful to him. It is the wrongdoers who will miss out big time in the end, whereas the 'right-doers' will receive their eternal reward.

There is wisdom and justice to be found on my tongue and stability in my feet when I am absorbing and meditating on God's word.

The bad people want to see an end to the good people, but God will not allow it - justice will be done.
So, I am going to keep putting my hope in the Lord and walking in his ways, for I know he will enable me to achieve my destiny.

Sometimes you see bad people flourishing like a healthy house-plant, but if you keep looking they will eventually wither away and be consigned to the compost heap. The future belongs to the Christ-followers, the 'good-doers' and the peacemakers. There is no future for those who reject Christ or for the bad people of our world.

I am fully aware that my eternal salvation has come from my Lord and he is also the one to whom I can find physical salvation in times of trouble. He helps me, delivers me and saves me as I take refuge in his heavenly castle.

Psalm 38

Lord, I need your mercy rather than your judgement right now. It feels like you have an angry hand weighing heavily upon me, somehow drawing health away from my body. My very bones ache within as the realisation of my sin seeps inwards. I am bent over with guilt, it is like carrying a heavy sack on my back. The physical consequences of my sin are obvious to all. I am very depressed. My back muscles are in constant spasm and I feel a physical wreck. I am weak, defeated and heart-broken.

You know what I am longing for; my inner being is like an open book to you. O Lord, listen to my pounding heart, feel my failing strength and look into my lightless eyes. Even those close to me are avoiding me because of all this; my neighbours are not calling in anymore. As for those who would like to see the back of me, well they are scheming and looking forward to my complete downfall.

I feel like a deaf mute – I am not hearing anything and I can't talk any sense. So what can I do? Lord, I will wait to hear from you. I don't want people to gloat over my downfall. I know I am on the way down – it is so painful right now – this sin is the source of my troubles. Lord, I confess my sin to you.

The numbers of those against me seem to be escalating for no apparent reason. Some even repay my good with bad and mount false allegations against me. So Lord, I am asking that you will stay close. Please come quickly and help me, for you are my Lord and my Saviour.

Psalm 39

I was determined to keep examining the way I was living and what I said. I realised that particularly when there are people around who will twist what I say, it is most important to be economical with my words. However, when I didn't say anything or do anything, not even anything good, the turmoil within me increased. My inner being began to burn and I had to speak.

Lord, I ask that you would give me a glimpse of the end of my life and how short it all is really. Help me to appreciate each day and live more in the now. The length of my life is like a pin-head compared to eternity, like a breath that causes some condensation on a glass and is then gone.

People are like leaves blown here and there in the breeze as they go about their everyday lives, but most of our bustling about doesn't get us very far. Some spend all their time amassing a sizeable fortune, but have little idea who will inherit it after their brief spell on this planet.

So, Lord, what am I looking for? I really need to be looking to you. Please save me from the many pits I am prone to fall into; I don't want to end up looking worse than a fool.

I didn't know what to say, for I realised that it was you, O Lord, who was allowing things to happen to me. It was like a warning shot from heaven and I was overcome by its severity. When you tell me off and discipline me for my waywardness, the materials I have accumulated can fast disappear, like a stolen car. I really do need to count my days.

Lord, please hear what I am trying to say to you, listen to my plea for help - do not turn away from my tears. It feels like we are strangers. I know this is not true, but it seems like it would be better for you to turn away from me; perhaps then I would enjoy life again before I die.

Psalm 40

At peace, I waited for the Lord to come to my aid, to hear my cry; and then he did. He lifted me out of my well of despair, out of the mud of my circumstances that prevented me from going anywhere. He then placed me on a concrete path – a place where I had a sure footing. I found myself singing praise songs again.

There are going to be so many who will find the Lord and start putting their trust in him. How blessed are those who trust God rather than those who think they have got it made or those who worship materialism.

Countless are the wonders God has performed and many are the things you have planned for me. No-one and nothing comes anywhere close to you and if I started trying to tell someone of all you have done it would take me more than a life-time.

You are not so much interested in any sacrifices I might make for you as you are in spending time with me, speaking to me. You are not so much interested in what I can offer you as you are in me as a person. It is relationship you are after and so I don't feel burdened to serve you; I serve you because I want to, because that desire is etched into my heart.

I will share my testimony in church of what you have done; people need to know. I won't keep hidden how good you are, but let others know about how faithful you have been and how you have helped me. I won't keep hidden your amazing love and faithfulness.

Lord, keep your mercy flowing towards me, your love and faithfulness surrounding me, because troubles are queuing up to attack me and sin can so easily overcome me. There are so many troubles out there that I can't count them and my health is suffering as a result.

So Lord, come quickly and help me. If there is anyone who wants to make my life a misery, would you expose them, confuse their plans and embarrass them.

May all who seek you be happy and full of joy; may they be able to shout, "God is great!"

As for me, I recognise that I am poor in spirit and needy of something greater than myself, so Lord, think of me. You are my helper, my deliverer, my God – come quickly Lord.

Psalm 41

When I take care of the weaker people in my community, God is pleased and will bless me. When I am in trouble God will deliver me; he will protect me and keep me safe. I will truly find God's blessing on my material life and those who are against me will be thwarted. God will help me recover from sickness.

Lord, have mercy on me - I know I am far from perfect – I really need your healing touch. People who don't like me are wondering when I am going to die and my name disappear forever. They come and see me and say the right things, but then go away and spread lies about me far and wide. They whisper amongst themselves and imagine the worst for me. They talk about me having an awful fatal illness.

Even my close friend, someone I trusted, someone who I have shared many meals with, has turned against me. So, Lord, will you have mercy on me. Raise me up from this sickness and then they will see I am not going to die just yet. I know you love me and find pleasure in me because in the end those who are against me never prevail. You honour my integrity and I find myself in the centre of your presence.

I praise you, Lord and will do so forever and ever. A double amen!

BOOK 2

Psalm 42

Like thirsty animals in the heat of the day desperately try to find water, so my soul longs to find you. My very soul is thirsty for the streams of living water that flow from your presence. I ask myself, "When can I get away from it all and be alone with God?"

I have been drinking my tears rather than your Spirit. People around me are asking where God is in all this. But now I choose to remember how, in more stable times, I used to go to the place where God's people assemble and joined in with all the shouts of joy and praise.

Why am I feeling so low? Why am I so disturbed inside? It's because I haven't been putting my hope in God, I haven't been praising him. So, because I am feeling down, I am going to make a conscious decision to remember you wherever I go.

There is something deep that is calling to the depths of me – it's strong, like the roar of a waterfall. I feel overwhelmed by the waves and breakers of life, but your love, O Lord, is being directed towards me in the day time; I can even hear you singing over me in the night time. I will turn that song into a prayer.

I say to God, the true rock of my life, why have you forgotten me? Why do I have to go about mourning and feeling oppressed? In fact, my very bones are feeling the strain of the voices within that taunt me all the time with the question, "Where is your God?"

Why am I feeling so low? Why am I so disturbed inside? It's because I haven't been putting my hope in God, I haven't been praising him. So, that is what I am going to do; I am going to put my hope in God; I am going to praise my Saviour and my Lord.

Psalm 43

Lord, help people see that I was right in what I said and did all along, after all, your cause is my cause and I live in a nation that is rejecting you. Draw me out of the tangle of worldly arguments.

You are a stronghold to me, so why do I feel like you have rejected me? Why do I feel so stressed by some of the people around me?

Lord, shine your light on my path and lead me back into your glorious presence. In your delightful presence is joy and peace, it is there I will praise you and declare again and again that you are my God.

Why am I feeling so low? Why am I feeling so stressed? I haven't been putting my hope in God. So that is what I will do, I will put my hope in God my Saviour and I will praise him.

Psalm 44

Lord, I know the Bible well, the stories of what you did long ago; the victory of your people over their enemies and their successful planting in a foreign land. You enabled them to flourish there. It was you who enabled them to win against all the odds. It was your hand, your power, your face shining upon them, because you loved them so much.

You haven't changed. You are my God, you are my King and you declare victory over my life. It is through you that I am able to push through all that is against me; it is by declaring your name that I will conquer my foes.

I will not put my trust in my own ability, for that will not get me through. It is you who will get me through – it is you. I will make sure people realise that it is you and I will praise your name for ever.

Right now though, it doesn't feel like you are with me. It feels like you have turned your face away from me and are humbling me. I don't feel like you are going out ahead of me to bring me success in my exploits for you. In fact, I have retreated as a result from serving you in various ways and feel far from blessed. I feel abandoned by you, isolated and sold out. People I know laugh at me because I am a Christian, they shake their heads as if to say, "Why would anyone believe in God?" I sometimes feel like a second class citizen, a foreigner in my own country.

This is happening even when I am still following you. My heart is still in love with you, I am not doing anything bad and yet still there is this sense that you are crushing me, covering me with darkness.

I could understand it if I had forgotten you, or if I was worshipping something else – because you know the secrets of my heart. Yet, for your sake, I am facing this darkness and sense of abandonment all day long.

Lord, I am asking for you to notice me again, be active in my life, shine your face towards me, deliver me from my misery and oppression, raise me up from the dust, clean me up, help me, rescue me, just like you did in the olden days because I know you still love me - your love never fails.

Psalm 45

My heart is stirred by the Holy Spirit to speak out worship poems about Jesus.

For Jesus is the most excellent man that ever lived. He brought grace teachings from heaven as he was blessed by God.

O mighty Lord Jesus, would you send more of your Spirit to us. Come to us clothed with splendour and majestic authority and ride out victoriously on the wings of angels into our streets and communities bringing truth, humility and justice; may awesome things happen around us. May the enemies of righteousness be slain and nations come to know you.

You are going to reign forever and justice will be a hallmark of your kingdom. You love everything that is right and hate everything that is wrong; so your Father has elevated you above everyone and has gifted you with a deep joy.

Jesus, I am so looking forward to the Royal wedding, when you will return as the bridegroom and be united to your bride, the church. Your robes will be full of the fragrances of heaven and angelic music will make your heart glad on that day.

You will have eyes for none other than your royal bride, the church, who will be at your right hand dressed in pure gold.

Listen, you bride to be, make sure you are keeping watch for your bridegroom, putting aside distractions. Let your kingly groom be overcome by your beauty; honour him, for he is Lord.
Cities will be given to you as gifts and prosperity will follow you forever.

How glorious you will be with your gown interwoven with gold, your robe embroidered with the good works of God's people, as you are led to your King. What joy and gladness there will be as you enter into his very presence and see him for the first time.

Your inheritance will be a new earth and you will reign with him forever. Praise will always be on people's lips forever more.

Psalm 46

Lord, you are the one I can go to at any time, but particularly in times of trouble, and find safety and strength. For this reason, I will not fear, whatever is happening around me. Even if the very foundations of my life are shaking and the wild forces of nature are raging near me, I will not be afraid because your Holy Spirit brings peace and joy to my innermost being, the place where you dwell.

You are right there within me, so I know I will not cave in under the strain; you will help me face tomorrow. Nations may be at war, countries overthrown, but when you speak nothing can fight against your word.

Oh, how comforting it is to know that the Lord Almighty is with me and is like a castle for me.

There is coming a day when the Lord will intervene in our world, once and for all. He will bring to an end all unrighteousness and wars will stop. Even the weapons of war will be destroyed.

But now he says to me, "Be still, quieten your soul, and know that I am your God." He also reminds me that one day he will be exalted in the whole earth. It is this almighty God that is with me and who is like a castle for me.

Psalm 47

I want to clap and shout with joy to the Lord. Lord, you are truly awesome; you are the great King over everything. You have given me victory over opposition, opened doors for me to progress towards your promises for me.

May you be lifted up with my shouts of joy and the music resounding in my heart. Oh may I sing your praises - much praise to you my King. You are the King of all the earth – that in itself draws praise from my soul. From your heavenly throne, you reign over everything. One day, all nobility will bow before you, because the whole earth belongs to you and you will be greatly exalted.

Psalm 48

Lord, you are so great and most worthy of my praise wherever I am. You have made your dwelling place within my innermost being. I am also a living stone in the greatest of temples. How beautiful is the spiritual house you are building, how magnificent; it is the joy of the whole earth.

You are right there protecting your worldwide church, you are our fortress.

There have been many attacks from many aggressors in most countries over the last centuries, but still your worldwide church grows. May the enemies of your dwelling place be defeated in their attempts to discredit and destroy. You will make your spiritual house secure forever.

I am grateful for the ability to meditate on your unfailing love within your spiritual house. It is good to remember that your name and your praise, O God, reach to the ends of the earth. Wherever you are praised, righteousness will flow from your presence. I am so glad that you are the ultimate judge of all the earth.

When I contemplate this great global spiritual edifice that you are building and the price of the Living Stone who is its cornerstone, I am compelled to make sure my generation and the next know about it all. God, you are my God forever and ever; you will be my guide to the end of my days.

Psalm 49

Because of my relationship with the Lord and my meditation of his word, particularly his proverbs, I find that my words often provide wisdom and understanding to all sorts of people I talk to, whether they are important or ordinary, rich or poor.

I have put some of what I have learnt into a song:

Why should I fear when things go wrong,

When people try to deceive me?

They may trust in their wealth and boast,

But where do they go when they die,

Yes, where do they go when they die?

Is there a redeemer for their soul,

Someone whose paid the ransom?

How costly is the ransom price,

Would any payment be enough?

Enough for someone to live forever,

Yes, enough for someone to live forever.

All know that all die,

The wise and foolish together.

And all that they had and all they were worth

Means nothing to them in their tombs

Yes, means nothing to them in their tombs.

Will their tomb be their house forever?

Will dust be their endless fate?

Though they land and wealth amassed,

Will not they still endure somehow?

Oh, will not they still endure somehow?

For those who trust in themselves
Their fate is the same as the beasts.
Like sheep that are destined to die,
Like sheep without a shepherd,
Their form will decay in the grave
Yes, their form will decay in the grave.

But for those who trust in the Lord
There is a redeemer of the soul.
The costly payment paid in full
Enough for someone to live forever
Yes, enough for someone to live forever.

A heavenly mansion has been prepared
And Christ shall come again
He will raise me up from the dead
Yes, he will raise me up from the dead.

So what do I learn from this? I learn not to be overawed when others become rich and when the sizes of their houses increase. For they can take nothing of this with them when they die. Nothing of their splendour will go with them. They may have counted themselves fortunate when they were alive and may even have thanked God for their prosperity, but all along they missed the point - that God desires relationship with us which can only come through believing that Jesus paid the price for that.

Wealth without this understanding is meaningless. Without this understanding, wealthy people and poor people alike will eventually perish just like the animals. Once they have died, they will never see the light of life again.

Psalm 50

There is no-one who is as mighty as the Lord God. He can speak and make commands over the whole earth and it is still done, as it was in the beginning.

From the great heavenly city, God shines with pure beauty. But God is going to step into our realm once again and it won't be a quiet event! A raging fire will surround him and go before him.

He will summons all the people, those in heaven and those on earth together, that he may judge them.

I know I too will be at this judgement day. I am aware that I will stand before him as one who was cleansed of my sin, not through my sacrifice, but through the sacrifice of Jesus. The angels of heaven shout

out the righteousness of God twenty four hours a day for he is truly a God of justice.

I wonder what God might say to me? He may start by reminding me that he is my God. That is an awesome thought. He could remind me that he has nothing against me concerning the sacrifices I have made, although anything I have sacrificed came from him initially anyway, for the world is his and everything in it belongs to him. He might be pleased with my worship and thanksgiving, the promises I have kept that I said I would and my faith in him on those days of trouble. However, I will only be delivered by my faith in Jesus and oh, how I honour you for that.
What God says to the bad people will be a different matter.

He will remind them that because they rejected it, they have no right to God's new covenant through Jesus. They hated their makers instructions, cast aside his life giving words. They joined in with the bad practices of their friends, those who stole and had habitual illicit affairs. They spoke evil of others and lied through their teeth, even about their own flesh and blood. They thought God's silence was condoning their activities, but now they realise judgement day has come.

It is wise to consider all this. If we forget God and his salvation plan, God will eventually forget us. There will be no rescue from the torment of hell.

However, if we remember God and give thanks to him for his salvation plan that makes us blameless before him, then he will remember us and bring us home.

Psalm 51

O Lord, surely this time I have really blown it. All I can do is cry out for your mercy and appeal to your love that never fails me. Please show me your amazing grace and rub out my transgressions from your ledger. Like a fast flowing stream, wash away all my sin so that I will once more be as clean as new.

I know I have messed up big time, my sin is always staring me in the face. I know I have actually sinned against you, O Lord and what I have done is staring you in the face too. You are perfectly justified in bringing a guilty verdict against me.

From the very moment I came into existence sin has been developing within me, but even in my mother's womb you were looking for my faithfulness, as the basic foundations for wise living were being forged in that hidden place.

Clean me up with the sacrificial blood of Jesus and I will be right again; wash me, and I will be whiter than freshly fallen snow.

Then I will be able to experience joy and gladness again and my crushed spirit will be able to sing.

Lord, stop looking at my sin and look instead at Jesus, who removes the guilty verdict by paying my debts.

Now I ask that by your Spirit you would purify my heart and renew a determined spirit deep inside me. I could not bear to be removed from your presence, or survive without your life giving Spirit within me.

O, restore that joy of knowing I belong to you and put a willing spirit within me, so that I stick to the straight and narrow path.

Only then will I qualify again to teach other sinners your ways and help them on their journey back to you.

Only you can help me get over the guilt I feel, O God, my Lord and my Saviour. And then, I will be full of songs about your righteousness, so open my mouth, Lord, for out of it will come shouts of praise.

Right now, with my sin before me, you are not really interested in any sacrifice I might make, or offerings I might bring. No, what you are looking for is a broken spirit and a contrite heart; this is what means the most to you.

May I ask that you bring peace into my heart (your dwelling place) and build up my defences. Help me get on the altar again, offering myself as a living sacrifice and then help me stay there. I think that will bring you pleasure and that is what I want to do.

Psalm 52

Why is it that some people like to boast about the bad things they have done as if they are some kind of hero, when in fact they are a disgrace as far as God is concerned. Such people are forever telling lies and working out ways to hurt others. Their tongues are as sharp as razor blades, carelessly cutting people to pieces. They much prefer to do bad things, than good things; speak lies instead of truth. They take real pleasure in seeing people hurt by their deceit.

I am sure there will come a time when God will intervene in their lives and they will receive their just desserts. A time when their security will disappear and they will find themselves uprooted from what they know into a place of obscurity.

The good people look on from a distance and shake their heads. "Here was someone," they say, "who didn't put God first, but instead trusted in their own riches and grew strong by manipulating, using and destroying others."

There, but for the grace of God, go I. Because of his grace, I have become like a fruit tree, flourishing in God's presence. I have come to trust in God's unfailing love for me. Wow, that love will go on forever and ever.

O Lord, I am so grateful for what you have done in my life and I will always be full of praise, especially when I am with other like-minded people.

My hope is in you, for you are 100% good.

Psalm 53

I have often thought how unwise it is to be an atheist and actually declare that there is no God. If God is completely taken out of the equation of our lives we have no moral compass, which can lead to all sorts of corruption and bad practices. Put simply – No God, no good. God searches the planet to see how many understand that he must exist and are searching for him.

Sometimes it seems like there is no one in that category, that everyone is pursuing life without God, becoming corrupt and selfish as a result.

Surely there must be some who know something about God and yet they eat God's people for breakfast; they never even think about communicating with God.

Nevertheless, they are drowning in fear, when that would not be necessary if God were in their lives. The tragic thing is that their ashes will one day be scattered with no hope of eternal life.

I pray for salvation, for revival, that Jesus will finish building his church and we will be able to dance for joy. Amen.

Psalm 54

Lord, once more I am in trouble and need rescuing, so I am calling out to you and asking that you will defend me by your great strength.

Here is my prayer, so please listen as I speak it out:

There are some people who think they know it all, trying to bring me down and ruin me. They are not consulting you on the matter. However, I know that you are my helper and you will sustain me through this.

The tables will eventually turn on those who speak ill of me and no-one will take any notice of them anymore.

I will freely and willingly offer my life as a living sacrifice to you. I will praise you, for you are so good. You have been my deliverer in my times of trouble and I have had the privilege to rejoice as you got me through to more peaceful times.

Psalm 55

O God, please listen to my prayer, may my desperate requests get to your ear and may I receive an answer.

My mind is a mess and I am a mess, because of what people have said and because of their threats. My health is beginning to suffer because of all this; these people are so angry.

My emotions are a mess and I even wonder if I will die. I am full of fear, trembling within – it is like being in a horror movie, only it's real.

I have thought to myself, if only I had wings, I could just fly away to some far-away place and rest awhile. I could go anywhere, somewhere completely deserted, and I would be sheltered from this storm that is raging around me.

Lord, would you confuse these people who are messing up my life and confuse their words, so they make no sense. There is a lot of violence and conflict in the community, whether it is day or night.

People are always looking for ways to harm and abuse others. It's a destructive force at work. Threats and lies are endemic.

If it was an enemy who was insulting me, I could take it. If it was an adversary coming against me, I could run and hide. But what really hurts is that it is my close friend and confidante, the person I used to pray with and worship next to.

This is the work of the evil one and I stand against him and his cohorts with shield in hand and pray for victory in the name of Jesus. For as I call out to the Lord, he saves me. I am crying out morning, noon and night in distress and he is hearing me. He will rescue me unharmed from this battle, despite the numbers who are against me.

My God is the eternal King who never changes and as these people who are against me have no fear of God, he will humble them because of their arrogant words.

I still can't understand why my friend is attacking his friends – destroying long built bonds. His talk is smooth, but his heart is hostile. His words are slick but they are like a loaded gun.

I am going to bring all my cares to the Lord and he will keep me going. When I do this, I will never be shaken up.

I know that God is the judge and he will deal with the rebellious people in the most just way.

As for me, I am going to put my trust in the Lord.

Psalm 56

O Lord, I am in need of your intervention in my life right now. I have some people hot on my heels pressing in for an attack. I am worrying about it all the time. They are so arrogant they believe they are absolutely right to pursue me in this way.

I admit I am afraid and so I must put my trust in you. When I put my trust in you and the words you have spoken, I find my fear melts away and I start to see things in perspective. These people are mere humans and powerless compared to you. They may twist my words and make plans for my downfall. They may conspire and watch my every step hoping for that opportunity to finish me off.

However, I will put my trust in your justice, O God. I will wait for you to bring this persecution to an end.

I know you are recording my anguish in your memory banks, every one of my tears you individually count. As I call out to you for help, my tormentors will be thwarted and I will know once more that you are for me.

Your words and promises are so praiseworthy and they keep me going as I put my trust in you. I don't need to be frozen out by fear, I mean, what can mere human beings do to me?

I have made a covenant with you, my Lord and I will now bring perfuse thanks to you in prayer; for you have delivered me from the darkness and my feet from stumbling on your path. I can now continue my life-walk with the Lord as he lights up my way.

Psalm 57

O God, I am looking for your favour to be upon me as I take refuge in you; as I take refuge from the storm in the huge shadow your wings cast as light cascades from your presence.

My cry will be to you, the Most High God, who will clear my name. Who will send angels from heaven with packages of love and faithfulness to save me and put to shame those who are against me?

It feels like I have been thrown into a dangerous lion enclosure, except the lions are people with mouths that can bite your head off and tongues that are as sharp as a carving knife.

In the midst of this I will praise you – be exalted, O God, to the highest place of honour and may all your goodness fill the world.

These people tried to trip me up and I was feeling the weight of the opposition. They set a trap along my path, but they have fallen into it themselves!

My heart is sticking to you like glue, like good quality glue. I am going to break out in song and compose some music. Come on, soul, wake up and get going! Let's make some loud music early in the morning that will wake everybody up!
I am full of praise to you, O Lord, and I will be singing your praises wherever I go. Your love is so great, it knows no bounds and your faithfulness is sky high.

Be exalted, O God, to the highest place of honour and may all your goodness fill the world.

Psalm 58

Politicians and nation leaders may have justice in their talk but do they have it in their walk? Do they treat all people the same? No, their hearts are full of injustice which overflows into their actions across the world.

The capacity to sin, even when very young, is cavernous in some. Lying is a way of life. Their tongues are poisonous and they simply don't care what damage they do. No-one, not even the best negotiators, can tame the tongues of these people.

But you can do it, Lord. You can remove their bite. You have an antidote to their poison. You can cause their influence to become insignificant; their sharp words to fall on deaf ears.

You can make them melt away like snow when the sun comes up – people of no consequence – swept away in the current of your power. Those who champion the right causes will be pleased when these people are out of the way, when they can step over them and get on with their kingdom work.

They will be able to say, "Good will always triumph over evil, because God is good and he is the judge of all the world."

Psalm 59

Lord, I need you to send your cavalry to save me; to be my defence against those who are attacking me.

Save me from the bad people, from those who want to see my downfall.

They lie in wait for me, conspiracy within their hearts, and yet I have done them no wrong. There is no sin or offence that I have committed that justifies their attacks. So, Lord, please come quickly to my aid; see my dilemma.

Lord, you are the almighty God, my God. So, will you rise up and bring justice to bear here, justice is all I ask. For these people keep turning up like a bad penny, intimidating me wherever I go. Poisonous words pour from their mouths and they don't even think about whether you are listening to them. However, you do hear them, and you are not impressed!

I reaffirm to myself this day that you, Lord, are my strength and I am going to keep a look out for you. You really are like a castle to me, my God on whom I can fully rely. God will go before me and I will be able to see an end to all this slander against me. Lord, you are sovereign and I will leave their fate in your hands, but I would ask that they will be caught out in their pride, because their words, their curses, their lies, are so damaging. These people need to be stopped before they hurt anymore people. So, may your reign be seen in this situation, Lord.

These people keep turning up like a bad penny, intimidating me wherever I go. Like a stray animal ravenous for food, these people are hungry to hurt.

However, I will rejoice in your strength and every morning I will sing of your love. You are my castle, my refuge from the storm. You are my strength and I love to praise you. You really are like a castle to me, my God on whom I can fully rely.

Psalm 60

A prayer for Wales (UK) – a prayer that can be adapted for any nation.

Lord, sometimes it feels like you have rejected this tiny nation of Wales; that you have been angry with us and withheld your blessing. Well, will you now restore this nation back to you?

This land has been shaken and torn apart by tremors of neglect of you. It is still quaking. Will you come and mend the fractures in our society. Loss of industry and financial austerity has led to desperate times. Some have turned to life controlling substances to mask the deep problems within.

However, those who love you Lord, are raising a banner upon which is the crest of Jesus; a banner that brings fear to the enemy of our souls.
Save this nation, Lord, help us with your mighty hands; may your church be delivered from its oppression.

I hear God speaking from his throne-room:

"In triumph I will reclaim Abergavenny and bring back the Valleys into my possession. Newport is mine, Swansea is mine; Anglesey is my helmet, Cardiff is my sceptre. Aberystwyth is my washbasin; on Milford Haven I throw my shoes; over Newtown I shout in triumph."

Who will bring us to the fortified strongholds, who will lead us to the Caernarfons? Is it not you, O Lord, you who seemingly have rejected us and no longer fight for us? O God, we need your help against the enemy, for our human strength is futile. With you Lord, we will certainly gain victory and you will trample underfoot the enemy of the soul of this great nation of Wales.

Psalm 61

Lord, hear my desperate prayers. It feels like you are a long way off and my spiritual tank is very low. So, will you lead me to the place of your presence, that place which is so much higher than where I am right now.

You have always been my defence mechanism against the enemy of my soul, the person to which I can run. How wonderful it would be to spend all my time in your presence, continually finding shelter under your wings.

I know you remember my promises to you and you have kept your side of the bargain.

Lord, may my earthly life be long, blessed by your love and faithfulness, but more importantly, may I find myself wrapped up in your presence both now and forever. From there, I will be full of praise songs and will be more able to keep my promises to you - day after day.

Psalm 62

It really is true, my inner world finds peace in God and he is my saving grace. It really is true that God is a rock on which I can stand, a wooden cross from which I am saved and a castle in which I can be safe – this makes me earthquake proof!

There are some who are against me, who try to intimidate me to bring me down. They sow lies and are two faced. But I find my peace in God, he is where my future lies. It really is true that God is a rock on which I can stand, a wooden cross from which I am saved and a castle in which I can be safe – this makes me earthquake proof!

My very life and reputation are in God's hands - he is a huge brick to whom I can run to. Whatever the circumstances, I can trust him, pour my heart out to him, escape to him.

It doesn't matter what class we were born into – we are all pretty insignificant in ourselves. Some try to make something of themselves through extortion, others by stealing. They think money will make them happy. Not so.

If we want to exercise legitimate power and enjoy unconditional love – we need to go to their source – God. If we get this right – God will reward us eventually.

Psalm 63

The one and only God is my God. It feels like I am in a spiritually dry place right now and I really need to get back to God. I am so thirsty for the living water of his Spirit, it is like my whole body is spiritually dehydrated and yearning to drink again from the river that flows from his presence.

I know what it is like to be in his presence, to feel his power flowing through me and his glory surrounding me.

There is nothing better than his love, not even life itself; for this reason, I will sing and praise him, I will praise him with hands lifted high for the rest of my life.

It is so satisfying getting into God's presence, it is like the feeling you get after eating a gourmet meal. No wonder I am full of praise. There have been times when I have spent the night praising and praying, because God is my helper. I can shelter in the shadow of his wings. I can cling to him and know that he will hold me up.

There are those who want to get rid of me, but God's justice will shine through eventually. Liars will be silenced by the truth.

As for me, I will find my joy in God and I know that all who do that will be blessed.

Psalm 64

Father, hear my prayer. I have a problem with the enemy of my soul. His schemes are all around me threatening my life. Deliver me from his demons which conspire and plot against me. They use people to speak sharp words and fire accusations like bullets from a gun. They are good at sneaking up and surprising me with sarcasm and false praise. They cause others to join in through gossip and set traps hoping I will fall into them. Their plans are full of injustice and yet they think they are perfect.
How deceitful human beings can become!

But you, O Lord, are on my side to help me in this battle. Your arrows will win the day. The lies of the enemy will be seen for what they are and others around me will know I have been vindicated.

When God's victory is clearly seen, people will take note and begin to respect him. They will think and testify about what God has done.

Those who have been made righteous through Christ can always find joy in the Lord, can always take refuge in him and can always find praise for him in their hearts.

Psalm 65

Song 1: You forgave us.

Praise from our hearts has leapt
For you have answered prayers
To you our promises are kept
As others come with cares

When sin overcame us
You forgave us
Oh you forgave us
Of all our sin.

Song 2: The abundance of God's House.

Happy are those you choose
Those brought near to your throne
We are filled with good things

The good things of your house

How awesome and right are
The ways you answer us
You are God our Saviour
The hope of all the earth

Song 3: God cares for the land.

Your power formed mountains
You arm yourself with strength
You still the roaring seas
And the nations turmoil

The world is full of awe
Of wonders you have made
The dawn and sunsets both
Generate songs of joy

You have concern for land
You water and enrich it
By the streams you have made
The land brings forth its crops

This irrigation system
This land with its furrows

And plains and rains that soften
You, my God, ordained it all

There is a blessing and
There is a harvest and
There is an abundance
Due to your great wisdom

Even grass grows in deserts
Hills dressed to bring joy
Fields covered with livestock
Valleys adorned with grain

All these things shout and sing
They shout out praise and joy
They shout out praise and joy
They shout out praise and joy

Psalm 66

May the whole earth shout for joy to God!
May its peoples acknowledge his glory
And make his praise the best ever.

Let's say to God, "Your deeds are so awesome!

How great is your power, so much so that it makes your enemies cower!

What a great day it will be when every knee will bow before you and constantly sing praises to you."

Come on, people, come and find out what God has done for you, his incredible gift to all. He sent Jesus, so that we could be delivered from all our wrongdoing and the mess we make and enter into the promises he has for us. Come on, let's rejoice in our salvation.

He is going to rule forever by his great power. Even now, he is watching the nations and those that are rebellious will be held accountable.

May all peoples praise our God, may the sound of their praise resound all over the earth.

I am so grateful that he has saved me and kept me from slipping into oblivion.

You have tested me from time to time, refining me like silver in the furnace. There have been times when I have felt trapped and laden with a heavy burden. Sometimes people have walked over me. It has felt like I have been through the mill. But you have brought me through and out into a place of abundance. I am motivated to come to your house with offerings of praise and worship; to commit myself to the promises I made to you when I was in trouble. I will offer myself on the altar, as it were, and say, "Whatever the cost."

I will tell others of the good things you have done for me. As I praised you even in my distress, you heard me and came to my aid.

If I had harboured wrong desires, God would have waited before listening, but as it was he heard my prayer.

I just want to praise you, Lord, for not ignoring my request or withholding your unconditional love from me.

Psalm 67

May God's people know his grace and blessing, may he look our way, because we want his loving ways to be known all over the world, his salvation in every nation.

May everyone praise the Lord. May whole nations praise him. May all nations praise him. May they be happy and sing joyful songs because your government, Lord, is just – all people are treated the same – your guidance is wise.

May everyone praise the Lord. May whole nations praise him. May all nations praise him.

We know our God blesses us, he provides for us. May God bless us so much that everyone everywhere will see and want to bow their knees to him too.

Psalm 68

God, there is an enemy that needs to be eliminated, a foe that needs to flee. Would you rise up and blow him away - may his schemes melt away like ice-cream in the sun before even more people succumb to his temptations and perish.

I am so glad for the 'divine exchange' – Jesus has taken my sin and I have received his righteousness. This causes me to sing joyful songs to God and makes me truly happy.

O let's sing to God, let's sing praises to him, let's show him how much we adore him, let's rejoice before him – he is the Lord.

He was like a father to me when I lost mine, he provided for my mother and also brought someone who was lonely into our family. These are the sorts of things he does.

He rescues those captive to sin and holds a party in heaven for each one; however, those who dismiss the offer of eternal life will continue to live in their spiritual desert.

God, you have brought your people through their wildernesses and into your promises via the mount of crucifixion. It was here that the earth shook, the rocks split and the heavens became dark as God's law was fully met by the Christ.

You pour the rain of your Spirit on your people and we are refreshed. People are now coming into your kingdom where the poor in spirit are satisfied.

The Lord declares, "My kingdom come, my will be done on earth as it is in heaven." People all over the world proclaim it, the enemy flees, spiritual plunder is taken. Even while we sleep his Holy Spirit hovers over his people like a dove, bringing gifts worth more than silver or gold.

How awesome it is when the enemy is driven out of our lives and God reigns in us. We see things from a different perspective, giants are dwarfed, for God has chosen to live in us by his Spirit forever. And he is not alone for he has angels too many to number at his command. How awesome it is that Jesus stepped down from heaven to earth to dwell amongst us. He died, so that the devil and his demons could be captured and then, after ascending back into heaven he distributed spiritual gifts to his people that we might become more like him and help others know God's presence in their lives.

God is my Saviour. He has saved me from the consequences of my sin, namely eternal death, but also continues to save me from burdens too heavy to carry.

What a tragedy that some reject God as their Saviour and continue on their path to destruction.

In my mind's eye, I catch a glimpse of a heavenly assembly. It starts with God leading a procession into his throne room, the mighty, countless throng of God's people who have all been bought by the shed blood of Jesus. There are singers and musicians leading this great multitude in adoration and praise of God. The least in the kingdom are in the front, those who have accomplished much in their earthly lives follow. As I see this vast congregation, it causes me to cry out, "Oh God, how great you are – mighty and strong – how we need you now to demonstrate your power and intervene in our world as you have done before, so that heaven can be more populated and hell plundered. May demons be defeated and heads of state bow to you. There are nations that revel in war that need to be dispersed so that peace may come to their peoples. Oh, may all nations sing your praises, to you, the one who travels faster than light, who owns every inch of the universe and who speaks with such power, that whatever you say happens. I will declare the immense power of my God, I will bow before his awesome majesty. Oh God, strengthen me with your supernatural power that I may do all that you have destined me to do. I am full of praise to my God."

Psalm 69

Lord, the storm floods have come, the waters have risen and I am out of my depth. The water is too deep, my feet cannot reach the bottom. I cannot tread water for much longer and the water is foul. I have cried out to you for so long, I am about to give up. There seems to be no help from you and hope is fast dissolving in the mire.

For some reason, a reason I cannot fathom, there are many who plot my downfall. I have been falsely accused and required to pay for what I have not done.

Father, you know the truth, you know all about me, nothing is hidden from you. My concern is for those who put their hope in you, or are seeking you, but look at me and think – "Is it worth it?"

I soak up the persecution for the sake of Christ. I am even ostracised by my own flesh and blood. But I am so in love with you, so consumed with passion for your church that when you are insulted it feels like I am being insulted. People don't understand this passion, this intensity, the emotion I feel. Civic leaders don't get it and drunks make up songs about it.

So here I am, Lord, pleading for you to show your incredible love and favour towards me. Save me, rescue me, deliver me. Extend your hand and lift me from the waters, the floodwaters, the deep waters, the miry waters, before they cover me forever.

I need you to answer me, Lord. I have faith that your great love and mercy will reach me. I need your face to shine upon me quickly, for I am in deep trouble. I need you to draw close to me, rescue me, deliver me.

Because of what I have done people cause me to feel ashamed and disgraced. Their critical words have broken my heart and I have lost all confidence.

Sympathy is nowhere to be found, there is no one willing to put an arm around my shoulder. I have lost all appetite.

I feel like they should get a taste of their own medicine and then feel what it is like to be cast into a dark pit of despair.

Let them feel your displeasure, lead them into a desert, a place of isolation. Perhaps then they will realise what they have done – rubbing in your discipline like salt in a wound. Let them realise that their behaviour is no better than mine. Maybe they will come to their senses and find their way back to you.

God, will you protect me from further affliction and pain. I will still sing praise to your name and bring you glory and thanks. I know this brings you pleasure, far more than my money or service. In fact, it doesn't matter how little I have, I know when I seek God I find happiness and my soul lives. The needy cry out and the Lord hears them. He does not turn away from his children found in captivity to the world's enticements.

May all heaven and earth praise him, also the seas and everything that moves. God will build his kingdom, people will be saved and find their home there. The fullness of this to come will be the inheritance of all who love him.

Psalm 70

Lord, I need you and I need you quickly to save me from the situation that is arising. There are people who have plotted my downfall and I ask that you confuse them and put them to shame. May their scheming backfire so that others will see the kind of people they really are.

However, may those who truly seek you rejoice and be happy in you; may their hearts be full of the refrain, 'The Lord is great!"

But don't forget me, Lord. For I am feely spiritually poor and needy right now, and I need your speedy help. You, after all, are my helper and my deliverer.

Come quickly!

Psalm 71

I take my refuge in you, Lord. Please don't let me be put to shame. You always do the right things and here I am asking you to rescue me, deliver me, hear me, save me. To be that high rock in the stormy seas to which I can always find safety. Give the command, send your angels to save me, to place me on the rock, to keep me safe.

It is good to be able to call you 'My God'. You are my strong deliverer from all that would try to grab me and pull me down.

You have always been my hope ever since I can remember. I have always put my confidence in you and relied on you. I can't imagine ever not praising you. When people see me, they witness your activity in my life.

I have God songs filling my soul; songs that show you off.

I know you won't cast me aside when my hair turns grey and my strength begins to fail. The devil may try to finish me off with false accusations and lies. Telling me that I am finished, washed up and of no use to God or man. But God, come and whisper your truth into my spirit, so that the lies and accusations will melt away like snow in the sun. The truth is, I always have hope in you. Because of this, praise erupts more and more like a volcano inside me. I want to tell people the wonderful things you are doing right across the world every day, but I only know a tiny fraction of it all. But I can tell people some of it, your miracles, your love in action.

From my teens you have been revealing who you are to me and you have done some amazing things in my life – I have a testimony to share which declares your goodness. I am convinced your goodness will follow me all the days of my life and I will tell the next generation about how powerful you are and all you do.

The great things you have done fills the earth. There is no-one like my God. You may have allowed many troubles to come my way, but there is always restoration around the corner. Even from the deepest pit you will raise me up. You will dust me down and put your comforting arm around me.

I will praise you with whatever I can, because you are faithful. I will praise you with whatever I can, because you are holy.

My mouth is full of joy – the praising kind – for you are my deliverer. I will speak of all the wonderful things you do as long as I am awake, because you have defeated the accuser of my life.

Psalm 72

Jesus is my King and he reigns with justice and is adorned with righteousness. Justice and righteousness blend together in perfect harmony in him. Where he is king true prosperity flourishes, because this is the fruit of doing what is right.

My King is the defender of the weak and oppressed. He is compassionate towards the children of those in need.

My King will reign through all generations, night and day forever.

My King is like refreshing rain falling on my soul bringing abundance. He make me thrive.

My King will reign across the whole earth. Even the remotest tribes will bow before him. His enemies will be overcome. Unlikely nations will acknowledge who he is; heads of nations will bring him gifts. In fact, all kings will pay homage, all nations will serve him.

My King will deliver those who cry out with no one to help them in their need. He will be full of compassion for those heading to their grave. He will mount a rescue mission for the victims of oppression and abuse – they are so precious to him.

My King will live forever. All the wealth of the world belongs to him. My King will receive praise and glory all day long.

My King will bring life in abundance wherever he reigns. It will be like a full crop of wheat swaying in the breeze. Like rich mown grass, thick and healthy.

My King's name will last forever, it will continue beyond time. All nations will be blessed because of him and they will call him 'their blessing'.

Oh may my King be praised. It is he and he alone who does things that cause people to marvel. Praise his glorious name forever and ever. May the whole earth be filled with his presence, power, splendour and radiance.

A very big Amen.

BOOK 3

Psalm 73

I know that God is good to those whose hearts are pure. Yet, I almost came to doubt this, I nearly lost my faith. I looked around at those who arrogantly displayed their wealth and I envied them. They didn't appear to have any struggles. They were the picture of health and their bodies seemed finely tuned. The common burdens everyone else has to carry seemed to pass them by. They seemed to avoid diseases.

As a result they exude pride and will not shy away from violence if they think it is needed. Their hearts are callous and all sorts of sin results. In fact their evil imaginations have no limits. They talk about people like they are dirt, malicious talk, menacing. They say they have a place in heaven but their heart is only worldly. And people follow them and swallow their false philosophy, hook, line and sinker. They don't think God knows what is going on, in fact they question whether God knows anything. They are care free, becoming very rich with little regard for anyone else.

As I look at their wealth, I question whether it has been worth my while keeping my own heart pure and living a clean life. I seem to be afflicted with all kinds of problems, all day every day. I have never expressed such thoughts because I didn't want to lead anyone astray, however such things are difficult to understand. I was deeply troubled until I brought this into your presence in prayer. You revealed to me their final destiny.

What seems to be a solid path for them is actually a slippery slope towards destruction. The terrors of hell await. Their so called dream life will turn finally into a nightmare from which there is no escape.

As I thought about this, I realised how stupid and ignorant I had been. You are ever present in my life, you hold me, guide me and counsel me. My final destiny is with you in heaven. Even now, you place me in heavenly places. This earth is nothing to me without you.

My body may waste away and my heart may become weak, but God is my complete strength and will be so forever.

I fear for those who are far from God, who have rejected him as their saviour. Even though God does not want any to perish, those who reject his rescue plan through Jesus cannot be saved.

As for me, I know how good it feels to be close to God; to make the sovereign Lord my refuge. I will have many God stories to tell.

Psalm 74

Lord, it seems like you have rejected our land, your grace overlooking the cries of your people.

Our land has a rich Christian heritage, it's history littered with redemptive outbreaks. A land of God songs, where your presence transformed society. Would you do it again, turn your face towards our ruined land, towards all the destruction the enemy has caused, towards the empty chapels.

The powers of this dark world rage against us; they set up different standards; they cut down our young with devastating precision; they destroy our values; they put out the fire of your Spirit and impurity seeps in. They screech from their evil haunts, "We will get rid of them all." They targeted every place of Christian worship in our precious land.

Signs are in short supply, prophetic words seem hollow in our waiting for God.

How long will you allow this to go on for, Lord? How long will your name be just taken in vain? Why do you hold back? All you need to do is say the word and myriads of angels will be released to bring us victory.

God, you are King; you bring us salvation. Your power has no limits, even the mighty power of the great oceans are no match for you. You have the power to open up the ancient springs so that the streams of salvation can flow again. You have the power to stop the ceaseless flood of destruction flowing from hell.

Yours is the day and the night, for you created the sun and the moon. You created the atmosphere and established the seasons of our earth. The enemy sows foolishness liberally across the world and people say, "There is no God."

Like wild beasts, some seek the destruction of your precious lambs. Don't forget us, Lord. Remember that wonderful new covenant you made. The covenant that destroys the violence of the enemy and lights up the dark places. That sets the oppressed free and releases social justice to our lands, bringing praise to your name.

Would you rise up, O God and defend your kingdom cause. The foolish have no regard for you. They join forces to get rid of your name. Their voices constantly rise up against you.

Psalm 75

I just want to praise you. I praise you because I feel your presence. I praise you because of all the wonderful things you do.

The times are in your hands; the day of judgement is on your calendar. There are unseen forces of nature that threaten the existence of our planet, but you sustain all things.

It is pointless the arrogant boasting and those who disregard God trying to show they are strong and have no need of faith. They speak as if they know it all.

But no one from anywhere on this planet can exalt themselves above God. And in the end, it is God who justly judges.

He brings one down He raises another up. In His hand is a cup full of punishment ready to be poured out on all the wicked. They will drink it down to its very dregs.

I will sing praise to God forever, to Him who reduces the strength of the wicked to nothing but increases the strength of the righteous.

To him be praise and strength forever.

Psalm 76

A prophetic song

God is renowned in Wales;

it is here that his name is great.

He has established himself in the North,

He has established himself in the middle

He has established himself in the Valleys

He has established himself in the West

He has established himself in the South

He has established himself in the East

He has made his dwelling place in this green and pleasant land.

Here he broke the fiery darts of the enemy; the fear and the lies, all the dark weapons in hell's armoury.

O God, your radiant light now shines, your majestic rule covers every mountain like the morning mist.

Every demon lies plundered of its power, for Christ has triumphed over them; not one demon can lift as much as a finger.

For you rebuked them, King of our land, their horses and chariots lie abandoned.

Now there is no-one and nothing to be feared, except you. You were angry and turned over the tables of the enemy.

From heaven you proclaimed freedom, and the demons feared and fled— when you, God, rose up, all the lost of the land were saved.

Your wrath against the enemy has brought you praise, there are no survivors!

Wales has vowed to worship the LORD our God; let all the neighbouring lands do the same and bring their gifts of surrender to the One to be feared.

He breaks in pieces the rulers in dark places; he is feared by the rulers of the earth.

Psalm 77

O God, I am desperate for your help, once again.
I am crying out to you, please hear me.
I am so distressed.

I was so distressed that as I prayed during the night, I lay face down on the floor with my hands stretched out in front of me. Comfort seemed a long way off.

I tried remembering all God had done in my life and I inwardly groaned; as I thought about these things I began to feel weaker.

I couldn't close my eyes and I was too troubled even to speak.

I thought about the days when I had been so close to God and it seemed like years ago. I remembered the times when I would sing songs of praise long into the night.

As I meditated on these things, somewhere deep within emerged some questions:

"Will God reject me forever? Will I ever know his favour again? Has his unfailing love actually failed? Will his promises ever come to pass? Has God's mercy been exhausted? Is he so angry that he can no longer show compassion?"

Then some answers came to me:

Think about the years when God stretched out his hand towards me, the wonderful things he did, the miracles.

Come on soul, keep remembering God's activity, his incredible interventions.

God's ways are perfect and pure. There is nothing that compares to the greatness of God. The God who performs miracles. The God who displays his power. The God who redeems us.

Just as in ancient times when you rescued your people from the pursuing Egyptian army, you rescued me. As I passed through the waters of baptism there was a shout of victory in heaven as demonic forces of darkness were buried with me in the water. Your arrows destroyed them, your lightning struck them. Sin no longer had a hold on me. You made a way for my salvation and as I arose from the waters and my footprints left a trail on the ground, there was another invisible, divine set of footprints next to mine.

This is multiplied countless times over, as you continue to lead your flock through the waters into the land of promise.

Psalm 78

I often hear God speak to me. He likes me to listen. Sometimes he speaks in parables and reveals things from long ago. It is important that we pass on to the next generation the things we have heard and known about God; his deeds, his power at work, the wonders he has done. It is important that we teach our children the right paths laid down by God; the foundational truths we find in the Bible. And it is important that they in turn teach their children, so that God's commandments are kept from one generation to another, that each generation learns to trust God.

Otherwise, a generation will grow up that becomes stubborn and rebellious towards God, whose hearts are far from their creator, whose spirits are dead.

We see it today in Wales. The land of revivals, but in great need of another one. It's people have turned back from God, they have not walked in God's ways and have forgotten the new covenant of Christ.

They have forgotten the transforming things God has done, even before their very eyes. There were countless miracles that took place, people healed of all manner of ailments.

God intervened and provided a way through the sea of sin and led them to the place of safety from the enemy of their souls.

His Holy Spirit was given, bringing guidance as to how to live during the day and shining light into the darkness of night.

The living water of his Spirit flowed like a river in flood in the parched land, living water everywhere, even in the deep mines of the ground.

For years before the people of this land had been in rebellion against God, not trusting him. Not believing that God could do anything significant. The cry from the old Hymn rang out from the chapels and rugby stadiums, Bread of Heaven, Bread of Heaven, feed me now and forevermore.

God heard, his fire broke out and he commanded the doors of heaven to open and the Word of God, the grain of heaven, was poured out. This bread of angels became abundant and effective in relieving the spiritual hunger of the people.

God sent the wind of his Spirit that brought meaty sermons. Where once the Word of God was rare, now it was prolific, like sand on the seashore.

They fed until they were stuffed, like turkeys ready for the pot.

But it wasn't long before they turned away from God. The revival wave passed and people gradually returned to their spiritless selves. And so in spite of all that God did, only a remnant still believe.

O God, would you breath over this land again so that it does not end its days in futility and terror.

Would you pour out your Spirit again, so that people will seek you and eagerly turn to you again. That they will remember you as their Rock and Redeemer. That their mouths would be full of grateful praise and earnest truth. That their hearts would be committed to you and they will be a faithful people.

Would you pour out your mercy and forgive their sins, so they will be saved from the wages of sins and the destruction of hell.

Remember, O God, that they are only flesh and blood. A slight breeze that doesn't come back.

I know how much they have been in rebellion against you and caused you grief in this barren land.

They have repeatedly stretched your patience, caused you to look away. They have not remembered your power, the times when you have redeemed this nation from the grip of Satan. The days when signs and wonders multiplied through the land. When the cleansing blood of Jesus flowed like mighty rivers through the nation and they no longer had the desire to drink from the normal streams of sin.

When you sent angels to do battle in heavenly places overcoming the demonic forces of darkness. Releasing people from oppressive spiritual activity that devoured, devasted and destroyed them. There arose peace, prosperity and abundant life in the land.

God brought his people to a good place as a shepherd leads his flock to pastures green. The valleys once dark as coal dust, were now green with spiritual renewal.

With the demons drowned in the sea of God's spirit, his people were now safe and at peace. The land became holy, the enemies of God driven away. Here, the kingdom of God could be seen.

O God, I am sorry the people have continued to test your patience and have rebelled against you. They have not kept your commandments and by and large are disloyal, faithless and fickle.

I count myself as such at times, no doubt arousing your jealousy through putting other things above you. I thank you that you have not rejected me and I pray you will not reject this land, O God. Do not abandon us, do not cause your presence to leave us.

Many of your churches are in ruin or inhabited by those who do not worship you. Many of your people have fallen into the hands of our enemy.

The wrong fire has consumed our young people. The pastors are disillusioned.

O God, would you awake as a warrior ready for war. Would you once again beat back your enemies and show them up for what they are. Would you once again establish songs of praise throughout the land. Would the name of Jesus, our great shepherd, who, from humble beginnings has now been given the name that is above all names, be raised like a banner high over this land. May Jesus skilfully lead us again to the revival river.

Psalm 79

O Lord, atheism is invading your kingdom. In the West your church is being reduced to rubble, the places of worship are being compromised.
Your servant's spirits are dying, they have become the prey of complacency, the food of materialism. Your church is bleeding out, but few care about it.

The truth sticks in our neighbour's throats like fish bones and we find ourselves isolated from popular opinion.

How long will you allow this trend to continue, O Lord? How long before you send the fire of your Spirit to burn up our fickle behaviour.

How long before you show up atheism for what it is, ideologies that dismiss your very existence? Such things are devouring your people, devasting your church.

O God, would you forgive our sins and may your mercy be sent quickly to our aid for we are in desperate need.

You are our Saviour, O Lord. Come and heal our land for the glory of your name. Deliver us from the invading forces, for we are sorry for the weaknesses we have succumbed to. Forgive us for the sake of your name.

We don't want people to be mocking us with the question, "Where is their God?"

Right now, make known to those who say "There is no God," that you are truly alive. Will you stop the bleeding of your church, raise the spirits of your people from the dead, release the captives from the prison of despair?

May your church be seven times as strong as it ever was. May your powerful hand perform the miracle.

Then we, your people, your flock, will be full of praise, full of songs extolling your name. And this will continue from generation to generation, for ever and ever. Amen.

Psalm 80

Lord you are our Shepherd, we are your flock, please listen to us.

You are enthroned on the mercy seat, have mercy on us, O Lord, come with your shining glory into our land, so that we might be saved from our enemy.

May your power be awakened so that we might be saved from our enemy.

Restore us, may your face shine upon us, so that we might be saved from our enemy.

How much longer will we have to wait? How much longer until you answer the prayers of your people? Our food and drink have been our tears for so long, even our neighbours think we are mad; they taunt us without mercy.

Restore us, may your face shine upon us, so that we might be saved from our enemy.

You bought us with a great price from our sinful state. You drove out the demonic forces and planted us in your kingdom. The ground was fertile and the gospel seed took root and was fruitful. The gospel spread like wild fire across the earth.

But now, the kingdom feels like its boundaries have been compromised and the enemy is able to steal the fruit, wreak havoc and feed on the flesh of the weak.

Return to us, O Lord, take a look from your mercy seat and see what is happening. The fruitful vine you planted needs your tendering. The body of your Son needs attention. Pruning is one thing, cutting down and burning is another.

O, Lord, send the Spirit of your Son to revive us, then we will turn to you again with faithfulness and commitment. Restore us, may your face shine upon us, so that we might be saved from our enemy.

Psalm 81

Out of pure joy, I am going to sing, even shout out loud, to the Lord, who is my very strength.

Come on, let's begin the music, let's rattle some tambourines, let's start strumming on the guitars, get some melody going with the saxophone. It's a bright night, time for a festival.

Worship is part of my spiritual identity and if I do not do it, the stones around me will cry out instead. Ever since I was saved, worship has been forged as a statute on the walls of my heart.

God's Spirit whispers to my spirit, "Your sin burden has been lifted, you have been set free." The burden was heavy, I called to you and you rescued me. You answered like a bolt out of the blue. There was some bitter-sweet testing of my faith, but you are always faithful.

I need to be careful to hear what you are saying to me, to get into that place where I can listen to you. So many times you remind me that I should get rid of anything that gets in the way of my relationship with you, the foreign gods, so to speak, that I can so easily put in place of you.

You remind me that you are my God, yes, you are my Lord. You are the one who saved me from my sins. You are the one who feeds my soul. But so often I don't listen, I don't submit to you. Sometimes you leave me to get on with my own devices - my heart is so stubborn at times.

If I would only listen to you, follow your paths for my life, how quickly the demonic forces of darkness around me would be defeated. Not only that, but the soul harvest would be reaped much quicker and I will be filled with heaven's choice food and refreshed from the river of life.

Psalm 82

The injustice in our world causes God to speak out to those responsible:

"How long will you defend those who practice injustice, who give preferential treatment to evil doers? You should be defending the vulnerable and those without fathers. You should be doing all you can to help the poor and those oppressed. You should be rescuing the vulnerable and needy from the clutches of those who take advantage of them.

"Those who should know better, the rulers and governors in our world, know next to nothing, understand next to nothing of what some people have to go through. They are walking around in darkness whilst the very foundations of civilization are shaken.

"You rulers and governors, appointed by me, are failing in your duty. Remember you are mere mortals and will all die like everyone else."

O Lord, will you arise and bring justice into all the nations of this world, for it is all yours, your inheritance. (And help me play my part.)

Psalm 83

Lord, please speak, please hear, please draw near. The devil and his cohorts are making their presence felt. They conspire with all sorts of schemes against your loved ones. They are intent on destroying us without trace. They plot together with single mindedness. An alliance has formed from the camps of complacency, materialism, unforgiveness, immorality, pride, selfish ambition, anger, disunity, schisms, disloyalty and addiction.

Lord would you deal with them as you have done in the past. As you did in revivals of old, as you have done in various parts of the world from time to time. Would you bring confusion in their camps so that they will fight one another? Would you pierce them with the sword of your Spirit? Would you subdue them until they become a stench in the land? Would you make their heads roll; destroy them? These demonic forces have conspired to take possession of your kingdom, O God. So now, would you send your army of angels and make a public spectacle of them. May a violent wind from heaven blow them away. May your fire fall and consume them together with their evil schemes. May the river of your Spirit wash them away. May they never be able to show their ugly faces again; never be able to stop us seeking your name. May they be ashamed, dismayed and perish in disgrace.

May it be crystal clear that you are Lord, you alone are the highest authority on this planet.

Psalm 84

There is nowhere more lovely than being in your presence. It is what my soul longs for, there is a deep desire to be in that place. My heart shouts to my body above the distractions and says, "Let's get into God's throne room."

Even in the registered places of worship, birds find a home, ledges to build nests and have their young. These creatures enjoy the stillness of your presence in their chosen place of rest.

How happy am I when I am close to you, my mouth is full of praise to you, my Lord and King. How happy am I when I find my strength in you, when I have determined in my heart to get into your presence.

I might be going through a valley of life that makes me weep, but in your presence my tears turn to springs of hope and the gentle rain of your Spirit refreshes me.

I go from strength to strength the more I spend time with my Lord. So here I am Lord, please hear my prayers, lend your ear to my pleas, may I know your favour. I come before you as part of your family, as your child born again by your Spirit.

This I know, that it is better to spend just one hour in your presence than a whole year anywhere else.

I would prefer to be on the far-flung edges of your presence than live in the pompous splendour of the greedy. Because you, Lord God, are my light and my protection; it is you who gives me favour and honour; you have an open hand full of good things for me as I walk in your ways.

I am happiest when I put my complete trust in you.

Psalm 85

Lord, there was a time, long ago, when your grace was poured out on your ancient people and they returned to the land you had given them. You showed mercy and overlooked their sin. You put to one side the judgement they deserved, you looked upon them again with eyes of love.

That's exactly what needs to happen in our land now, Lord. The restoration of grace, mercy and salvation by our Saviour God. A national spiritual revival – it has been a few generations since the last one. Oh, how we will rejoice in you when it comes.

We know your love never fails, so Lord, would you demonstrate that love through causing a wave of salvation across this land.

Now is the time to listen to what God is saying – he promises us, his faithful people, peace. How important it is that we stay on his paths and do not deviate. I am convinced that salvation is close, that God's glory will be seen in our land.

When God's love and faithfulness are released, righteousness and peace covers the land. Faithfulness from the people springs up like wildflowers in the meadow and God looks down from heaven and is pleased. The Lord will throw out from heaven the gospel seed and the land will yield a great harvest.

A spirit of conviction goes before him and prepares the way for his activity.

Psalm 86

Lord, I am poor in spirit and in need of your enrichment, so please hear my prayer and answer it. I ask that you be my Guardian and Saviour as I endeavour to be faithful and put my trust in you.

What a privilege it is to call you my God and as I constantly cry out to you, please show your mercy towards me. Bring deep down joy into my heart as I put my trust in you.

O Lord, you are so forgiving and good to me. Your love knows no bounds! So, hear my prayer and my plea for mercy.

When I am distressed and call out to you, there you are with an answer. No worldly idol or god is like you, nothing anyone can do compares with what you can do.

One day, all the peoples of the world will come and worship you, Lord, they will praise and uplift your name above everything. For you are exceedingly great and all you do is marvellous to my eyes. You alone are God.

Lord, please show me your path for my feet, so that I can rely on you always being there. Give me an undivided heart, a heart that is wholly yours, a heart that reveres you.

I praise you, Lord, wholeheartedly and I will lift up your name always, because your love towards me has been beyond measure. You have lifted me out of the depths of despair, from the darkness of depression.
The enemy of my soul loves to attack me and his demons look for ways to destroy me. They hate you.

But you, Lord are so compassionate and full of grace, slow to become angry with me and your love and faithfulness know no bounds.

Lord, please turn your face towards me, may what I deserve never happen; may your power be seen in my life. Save me from the pitfalls around because I want to serve you faithfully.

Would you demonstrate your goodness towards me in such a tangible way that even those attacking demons will be embarrassed. You, Lord, are my helper and my comforter.

Psalm 87

The Church is like a city and God has established it like a city set on a hill. He loves the gate into the city, for it is Christ himself. Great things have been written about this city of God, for God himself has great expectations. Even those hostile to God will one day acknowledge this city, nations which worship other gods will say, "All these people were born in the city." Even those who do acknowledge God will say, "This person and that person were born in the city." God himself will build his city.

And there will be a book of life, a register of births. God will write in this book all who have been born in the city. The residents of the city will make music and will sing glorious songs. The city will have a fountain and all who drink from it will never thirst.

Psalm 88

A description of depression

Lord, you are my Saviour in times of trouble, so here I am crying out to you throughout the day and night. O, may my prayers reach your throne and may you turn your ear to my cry.

My problems are overwhelming, my life feels as if it is slipping away. It is as if my life counts for nothing. All my strength has drained away. I might as well be dead, lying in my grave, where you will forget me, where your care for me will cease.

Lord, you have allowed me to sink into the deepest pit where it is extremely dark. It is as if you are angry with me and that thought is like a heavy wave that overwhelms me. Even my closest friends don't want anything to do with me, they find me too difficult.

I am boxed in and cannot escape. There is no life in my eyes, only tears.

So, I am calling out to you, Lord, every day. Every day I lift my hands to heaven.

Lord, let me ask you some questions. Do those who are dead see your wonderful deeds? Are they able from their graves to praise you, or speak of your love and faithfulness?

Yet, here I am crying out for your help; every morning my prayers ascend to you. So, why are you rejecting me, why are you hiding your face from me?

From the time of my youth I have suffered, even been close to death. I have carried the burden of suffering for so long, I am in complete despair.

It feels like your anger has swept over me like a flood, pulling me under the water and causing me to drown. All who were close have abandoned me and now darkness is my only friend.

Psalm 89

Lord, I am going to sing about your great love not just now, but forever. I am going to talk about your faithfulness to anyone who will listen.

I will say, your love is firm and solid for all time and that your faithfulness is a spiritual law that can never be broken.

Long ago, you made a vow to King David that his descendants would always have a royal line. And I have become part of that line by being adopted into Jesus' family!

The angels in heaven praise your wonders, Lord, and I together with the multitudes that make up your church declare how faithful you are.

There is absolutely nothing in all the universe that compares to the Lord. The heavenly beings revere God, for he is more awesome than everyone and everything that surrounds him.

If I was to ask the question, "Who is like you, Lord?" I know the answer – no-one! You are the mighty one and your faithfulness is your mantle.

You are more powerful than the sea in a storm; when its waves become mountains you are able to bring calm.

You crushed the serpents head on the cross and all the demons were defeated.

O Lord, all the heavens belong to you, as does all the earth, for you created it and everything in it. You created the northern and southern hemispheres, both east and west rejoice at your wonderful name.

Your arms are powerful, your hands are strong. Everything that is right and everything that is just are built into the very foundations of your throne. Your love and faithfulness are like a fragrance that surrounds you.

I am so happy that I have learnt about you and can acknowledge you as my Lord. I am at my happiest when I am walking in the very light of your presence. I am able to rejoice in you all day long and celebrate how you always do the right things.

You, Lord, have become my beauty and strength and because of your favour I find myself full of courage. You are my defender and my king.

You spoke in visions long ago to your faithful people about a strong warrior you would raise up from amongst the people to be anointed king. His name was David. You sustained him, strengthened him and protected him so that his enemies did not get the better of him and evil people did not oppress him. The battles were not his but yours as you defeated his foes. Your faithful love was with him and you gave him much courage as he declared your name. He was able to conquer the land from the Mediterranean sea to the rivers in the East. Lord, may I also be a strong warrior for you. May I also cry out, "You are my Father, my God, the Rock, my Saviour."

There is such a link between David and Jesus. Jesus is your firstborn son and has been exalted with the title, 'King of kings'. The loving covenant you made with David to establish his hereditary kingship for as long as the heavens endure, found its fulfilment in Jesus who is now King forever.

Lord, you vowed that this covenant would be fulfilled come what may. Even if David's descendants did not follow your laws and ways, if they violated them and as a consequence had to endure your justice, still you would remember your love for David and remain faithful to your covenant. You cannot change what you have said, you are holy and cannot lie. You said his kingly line and throne would endure forever, just like the sun and moon which are faithful witnesses in the sky.

I know this has been fulfilled through Jesus. But there were times in Israel's history, when they doubted. They felt rejected and spurned. They felt you were so angry with them, that you had renounced the covenant you had made with David. His crown lay in the dust, the walls of Jerusalem were broken down, the strongholds in ruins. They had been plundered by their enemies and scorned by their neighbours. Their enemies became victorious and there was much rejoicing in their camps.

It was as if you, Lord, had turned your face away and removed your support in battle, putting an end to the splendour of the kingdom and throwing the throne of David away. The days of his kingship were cut short and he wore a mantle of shame.

Questions came flying to heaven, How long is this going to go on for, Lord? How long will you hide your face? How long will your anger burn for?

Sometimes things can look dark. We have received promises from God and there seems no way they can be fulfilled. We recall how fleeting our lives are, how futile life can be, how eventually we will die. We ask, where is God's love, where is God's faithfulness? Doesn't God know or understand what I am going through? The humiliation of unfulfilled promises?

But then I remember, that God is not in a hurry. That his covenant to David was fulfilled in Jesus. That even Jesus was (and still is) mocked and taunted and, at the height of his suffering on the cross, cried out, "My God, my God, why have you forsaken me?"

So, Lord, make me a strong warrior like David, help me follow in the footsteps of my Saviour.

I will praise you forever and ever.

A double Amen!

BOOK 4

Psalm 90

Lord, since the beginning of mankind, people have been enjoying your presence. Before a mountain was formed, before you created our wonderful world you were God and you will be God forever.

You formed us mortals from the dust of the ground and when we sinned you ordered us to return back to dust.

For you, Lord, a thousand years are like one swift day or like a few hours in the night time.

All of us eventually will fall asleep in our graves. We are like the new grass which springs up in the morning but by the time it gets to the evening we are dried out, full of wrinkles.

We can worry about your anger, even be frightened by it, as our sins that only we know about, lie exposed in the light of your presence. Do all our days fly under the shadow of your displeasure? Will our years simply finish with a sigh? We may live to seventy, or even eighty if we are strong, but is it not the case, that most of those years are full of trouble and woe? Where do the years go – they fly past and then we fly away!

There is no doubt that God's anger is powerful and we really need to respect that. We really do need to number our days, make the most of them, gain wisdom.

However, I know that the Lord sent Jesus to satisfy the just anger he had towards me because of my sin. He relented and showed great compassion towards me. His unfailing love casts away all fear and I am at peace. I am able to find deep joy in my heart that overflows into song every day. My momentary troubles and afflictions melt away in the joy of your presence for you give me the hope of eternal life.

May I experience your wonderful work in my life, may I appreciate your beauty. May your undeserved favour rest upon me and may all I do for you be successful - have your stamp of approval all over it.

Psalm 91

Those whose lifestyle choice is to be constantly aware of God's presence around them, will find peace as they rest in his mighty shadow.

I am able to confidently declare that the Lord is my refuge and my castle. I am able to put my complete trust in my God.

He will save me from the enemies traps and deadly diseases. Like an eagle that protects its young, he will cover me with his giant feathers and under his wings I will be safe. He will faithfully shield me. Fort Knox comes to mind!

So there is no need for me to fear anything! Nothing that may try to attack in the night time, nothing that may be aimed at me in the daytime. No dark disease or deadly virus. Many may die around me, but you will protect me.

I know that the wages of sin is death, but thanks be to God for the gift of eternal life through Jesus.

My trust is in the Lord. He is my refuge; his presence is my dwelling place, so how can any disaster come near me; any harm overwhelm me? Furthermore, there is a host of angels at God's command. He uses them to guard me in all my ways; they will lift me over dangerous obstacles, guide my feet around fatal hazards.

Why does God do all this? Because I love him and he loves me. The Lord says to me, "I will rescue you, I will protect you, because you confess your love for me. You will call out to me and I will answer. When you are in trouble I will deliver you from it and you will gain respect. You will live a long life and see my salvation plan running through it."

Psalm 92

It is so good to praise you, Lord, to sing out your name, especially when the church meets together. You are higher than anyone or anything. I delight in proclaiming your love in the morning and your faithfulness in the evening to music composed by so many talented people.

You make me glad because of what you do, Lord, your handiwork makes my heart sing for joy. So great are your works, Lord, and so profound are your thoughts!

All people need to know and understand that though bad people may flourish like the spring grass, their destiny is eternal death.

However, you Lord will be exalted forever.

There will definitely come a time when the devil and all his demons will be destroyed. Evil will finally be eradicated.

Lord, you have so strengthened me I feel as strong as an ox. You have anointed me with the fine oil of your Spirit.

My adversary the devil has been defeated by the death and resurrection of Jesus and all his demons have been routed.

I will flourish like a mighty oak tree, grow spiritually tall like a cedar, because I am planted and rooted in your house, O Lord. Even when I grow old, there will be fruit to bear as I stay fresh and watered in your presence. I will always declare that you, Lord, are upright; that you are my Rock; that you are perfect and holy.

Psalm 93

The Lord reigns and he is impressively majestic, impressively awesome and impressively strong. Just look at the world he created; it reflects his royal power and beauty.

Your reign had no beginning and will have no end. You are an eternal and infinite God.

When I look at the vast oceans, the towering waves of the deep seas, the pounding waves against the coastal rocks, the deafening thunder of the giant breakers on the shore; I think, "The King of kings made all this and he is mightier than it all."

Your moral laws like the physical laws you have put into place, stand the test of time. Everything about your throne room cries out, "Holy, Holy, Holy, is the Lord God almighty forever and ever." Amen

Psalm 94

There will come a time when those who have sinned will pay the penalty for their wrongdoing. Judgement day will come and God's punishment will be meted out. The unrepentant will receive the justice they deserve.

It doesn't seem fair that those who do evil things can be so jubilant. Their words indicate an arrogant attitude, they are full of boasting about their awful deeds.

They don't think twice about oppressing and annihilating your people. Their evil deeds extend to murdering the most vulnerable in society. They do not realise that you, Lord, see everything, nothing escapes your notice.

They need to come to their senses and put away their foolishness.

It is foolish to think that the God who fashioned the ear does not hear and he who formed the eye does not see.

It is foolish to think that the God who is able to discipline nations will not punish wickedness in individuals.

It is foolish to think that the God who gave mankind knowledge lacks knowledge himself. The Lord knows the plans of all human beings and he knows that compared to his plans they don't amount to very much.

Happy are the people you discipline, Lord, the ones you instruct with your ways, for they are spared much trouble, unlike the wicked who will fall into the pits they have dug for themselves.

The Lord will never reject his people; never abandon them.

Justice based on what is right in God's eyes is the way to go and those who walk in God's ways will be looking for that.

Social justice is a worthy cause to join – to stand up against the bullies of the vulnerable.

If God had not come to my aid, I would surely have entered an early grave. I felt my feet slipping from under me, but his love, which never fails, supported me.

When anxiety was getting the better of me, you consoled me and brought me joy.

Can a corrupt king who brings misery to his subjects become an ally of God? Of course not.

Wicked people form cartels and attack those who do right. They condemn innocent people to death.

I am so pleased that the Lord has become my castle, built on solid rock, where I can take refuge.

God will one day pay the wages of the sinful with eternal death. (But the free gift of eternal life is for all who repent and believe in the redemptive work of Jesus.)

Psalm 95

I am going to sing for joy to my Lord; I am going to shout out praise to Jesus, my Rock, my Saviour. I am going to come before him with thanksgiving and I am going to praise him with music and songs.

Why? Because the Lord is the one and only great God. He is the great King of kings. In his hands he holds the deepest parts of the earth and at the same time, the very tops of the mountains. The vast seas belong to him for he made them, his mighty hands formed the dry expanses of land.

So, that is why I am going to bow down in worship; I have to kneel before my Lord and Maker. He is my God and I am one of his sheep in his pasture, part of his flock under his care.

I can hear his voice today speaking tenderly to me, "Never let your heart become hard towards me. It can happen when things don't seem to be going well and you begin to doubt me – when you become spiritually dry. Remember my provision in the past, my guidance and plans working out in your life. Your salvation through Jesus. Don't be like my people in the wilderness whose short term memory loss led to their hearts going astray and who never reached the promised land. You know my ways and by my grace you will enter your rest."

Psalm 96

I feel like singing a new song to the Lord. Maybe the whole world could join in. I will praise the Lord day after day for his salvation plan in my life. Somehow I want everyone in the world to know about the radiant presence of God and his amazing deeds in every corner of the earth.

For God is so great and so worthy of praise; he is the One to be revered above everything and everyone. Many people worship gods that are lifeless idols, but I worship the God who made the universe! His majestic splendour radiates all around him; power and the brightness of his glory fill his throne room.

May every people, tribe and tongue bring God praise for his glory and power. May they give God the glory that is due to him; bring a sacrifice of praise into his presence.

I will worship the Lord in the splendour of his holiness, bow down and tremble before him. I will loudly declare, "The Lord reigns."

When God formed the world he made it to last and one day he will judge us all fairly.

Oh let the heavenly beings rejoice, let the earthly beings be glad; let the sound of the sea and everything in it fill the atmosphere with joy. Let the fields and the harvests bring the sound of jubilation; let the trees in the forests bring a chorus of joy. Let all God's creation rejoice before him, for at last he comes to judge the world. When he judges the world, he will do it righteously and he will be faithful to his promises.

Psalm 97

The Lord reigns from heaven, so let the world be glad, distant islands rejoice.

Thick clouds cover him; righteousness and justice are his foundational principles.

There is fire that comes from his presence and anyone approaching him who is not reconciled to him, cannot live.

The lightening that comes from his throne room lights up the whole world and when the people see it they tremble. Mighty mountains that rise up in the path of God, melt like wax before him.

The night sky speaks of all the wonders of God, we can all see his glory on display.

Eventually those who worship images and idols will find how futile that is, everyone should be worshipping him!

I am looking forward to the time when Jerusalem and the whole world will be rejoicing in the reign of God.

You Lord, are higher than anything or anyone in the whole world. You are raised up above everything people worship.

When we love the Lord and are faithful to him, we will hate sin as he does and he will guard our lives and deliver us from anyone who would want to harm us.

His light shines on those who do the right things and joy fills those with pure hearts. Rejoicing and praise flows freely from such people.

Psalm 98

I find myself singing a song never sung before in gratitude for the marvellous things the Lord has done. Due to his mighty power, his plan of salvation is working. He has revealed the redemption that comes through Jesus' death and resurrection to the nations. He remembered his love for the world and his faithfulness to his people and now all nations have been reached with the good news of Jesus.

So, come on world, let's sing together for joy to the Lord, let's spontaneously break out into songs of jubilation. Let's make some music to the Lord with whatever instrument we have to hand – guitar, trumpet, saxophone – let's sing from our hearts with the help of the Holy Spirit. Let's shout for joy before the King of all the earth.

May nature join in: let the sea's roar fill the air, let all that live in the sea – like whales and dolphins – add to the glorious sound. O, may the whole world and all who live in it join in. Let the rivers make their beautiful sounds and the mountain ranges echo with joyful singing. May all this produce a great symphony of jubilant praise as the Lord comes to judge the world. When he judges the world it will be done in just the right way and with perfect integrity.

Psalm 99

My Lord reigns from heaven, so may the nations of the world fear him. He is enthroned between the two cherubim, so may the earth itself shake.

My Lord is great, so may all the nations bow before him. Let them praise his greatness, his awesomeness and his holiness.

My King is mighty, he loves justice and impartiality. He has always done what is just and right in my life.

I am going to praise and honour the Lord my God and bow down in worship before him, for he is holy.

As part of your new covenant priesthood, as one who can hear your voice, I will call out to you and I know you will answer. You speak from the clouds of heaven and from your word – may I be found in obedience.

You are my Lord and you will answer me. I have always known your forgiveness and at times your discipline. I will praise and honour you; worship you in the most holy place of your presence, for you are my Lord and you are holy.

Psalm 100

I want to join with all the world and shout for joy to the Lord. I will worship him with a glad heart and get into his presence with joyful songs. For I know that the Lord is the one and only true God. He made me and I am his. I am one of his children, one of his sheep in his pasture.

I am going to enter his presence with a grateful heart and rest there, praising him; I am going to give him thanks and praise his wonderful name. For the Lord is so good to me and his love goes on and on forever. He is faithful and I know that will continue forever too.

Psalm 101

Lord, I love to sing you praise, particularly about your love and justice. I know I need to be careful about how I live my life – when will you come to me Lord?

I will try to make sure that everything that happens inside my house would have God's approval.

I will try to avert my gaze from anything that would not have God's approval.

I will try to lead a blameless life, for God hates sin.

I will try to choose my friends carefully because I don't want to get caught in the web of sin.

I will try not to engage in gossip and will not pass it on.

I will not have time for those who have an arrogant attitude and are full of self-pride.

I will keep close friendships with those who love you and spend time with them.

I will only allow Godly people to speak into my life.

I will avoid close friendships with deceitful, manipulative people and those who speak lies easily.

I will try to overcome evil with good.

I will seek to help those who do bad things transform their lives.

Psalm 102

O Lord, please hear my prayer, I am crying out for help. Do not hide your face from me, for I am in much distress. I need a quick answer, so please listen to my petition.

My days seem to be evaporating fast and what have I accomplished? The very fabric of my body is wasting away.

My heart is broken and all emotion is dying within. I am even forgetting to sustain myself with food.

I am so distressed, I find myself groaning aloud and my bones can be seen under my skin.

I am the picture of desolation, like the owl in the desert, perched in the ruins of a building.

I cannot sleep and feel sad like a bird that has lost its mate.

All day long demons taunt me, they laugh and whisper my name like a curse.

I sit surrounded by dust which has become my food and my tears are my drink. It feels like you, Lord, are angry with me, that you have thrown me aside and abandoned me. My life is like an evening shadow that quickly passes, like grass that withers away in the heat.

But you Lord reign forever, you are steadfast through all generations. I am sure you will arise and have compassion on your people. Surely it is time to show your favour, has not the day arrived that was marked on your calendar long ago?

The living stones of your church are treasured by your pastors, when they are missing it moves them to tears.

May the nations pay homage to the Lord, may all the heads of state revere your splendour and majesty.

The Lord will return in a blaze of glory and establish his kingdom. He will have compassion on the destitute and answer their prayers.

These words will be passed to a future generation, who will hear, believe and praise the Lord:

"The Lord will look down on the earth from his throne-room in the heavens and hear the groans of those held captive to sin - bringing freedom to those condemned to eternal death."

Then the name of the Lord will be declared on his holy hill and his praise will resound in the new Jerusalem as people from every nation, tribe and language assemble to worship him.

There was a time in my life when I was close to death, my strength was ebbing away. So I prayed, "Do not let me die, O Lord, for I am only in the middle of my normal lifespan.

"Your years are endless, Lord. In the very beginning you laid the foundations of the earth, you placed the stars and planets in their precise places.

"However, these created things are wearing out like everyday clothes. But there is coming a day when, like clothing, they will be changed - you will create a new earth and a new heaven, the former things will pass away.

"You will remain the same even then, you are an infinite God.

"Those whose names are written in the book of life will live in your presence forever."

Psalm 103

Let my soul cry out in praise to my Lord, let all that is within me praise him. O, may I praise the Lord and never forget all his blessings. He has forgiven all my sin, he heals my diseases, nothing is too hard for him. He has redeemed my life from hell; he has showered me with his beautiful love and compassion; his goodness towards me never fails, in fact, the older I get the younger I feel as he strengthens me.

I love the way the Lord is working out justice and what is right for those who are oppressed. He demonstrated this through the law of Moses and countless deeds amongst his people.

The Lord is compassionate, gracious, merciful and overflowing with love. He doesn't want to be constantly accusing people of their wrongdoing or keeping his anger on the boil. Jesus has provided the way to pay for my wrong doings, he has taken God's wrath open himself. Now, God does not treat me as my sins deserve – that's mercy; instead of paying me the wages of my sin, he gives me the undeserved gift of eternal life – that's grace. As infinite as the heavens are, so infinite is his love to me; further than the strongest telescope can see into space, so far has he removed my sin.

As a father has compassion on his children, so the Lord has compassion on me. He knows how he created man from the dust of the ground; that my life is as fleeting as the flowers in the field which flourish, but then the wind comes and blows them away and no one can remember where their place was.

Others may forget me, but not so with the Lord. For infinity, the Lord's love will be with me and the righteousness of Jesus will cover me. Because of this, I will endeavour to always walk in the ways of the Lord.

The Lord has already established his throne in heaven and from there his kingdom reigns. So may all the angels praise him, those mighty heavenly beings that carry out his instructions. May the vast multitudes of creatures that dwell in heaven praise the Lord. May all God's creation in heaven and on earth, in sky, land and sea, praise him.

Oh, let my soul cry out in praise to my Lord.

Psalm 104

Let my soul cry out in praise to my Lord, for you are extremely great and adorned with splendour and majesty.

The Lord robes himself in glorious light and then stretches out the heavens to form an infinite and breath-taking curtain. He builds his dwelling place on the clouds of the sky. The clouds are his chariot and he sours on the thermals of the wind.

His angels are sent on missions and he has the elements of the world at his disposal.

The Lord created the world and placed it in just the right place where it is firmly established. You covered it firstly with water that was so deep, it hid every mountain and then you spoke again with your thunderous voice and the waters started to move, vast currents developed and the waters flowed over the mountains, down the valleys to the places you assigned for them. Coastal boundaries were set and you promised to Noah after the great flood, that water would never cover the earth again.

The Lord has arranged springs to pour water into ravines and valleys which provide thirst quenching refreshment for all the animals. Some birds nest by these waters and sing their sweet songs among the branches.

He designed the great cycles of nature, arranging the rain to fall from the clouds to sustain the land which in turn makes the grass grow, that feeds the cattle, as well as watering plants that are cultivated for food, drink and cosmetics.

Trees too are well watered growing large and in vast numbers. Here the birds build their nests; the stork makes its home in the junipers.

The high mountains are the habitat of the wild goats and the rocky crags are home for the hyrax.

He made the moon which marks out seasons and the sun which he scheduled to rise and set. When it sets, darkness descends and the nocturnal animals awake to prowl the forests. The lions roar as they stalk their prey. The food chain that God designed is all in place. When the sun comes up, the scene changes and the animals of the night return to their dens to sleep. Now people are safe to go about their work until the evening.

Countless are the works of your hands, Lord! In your wisdom you made them all; the earth is bursting with your animals, the vast oceans teeming with living things, both massive and microscopic, we will never be able to count them.

On these waters ships are able to go about their business and sailors can watch the whales play.

All animals are ultimately dependent on you to sustain the balance of nature and their food chain. Like pets, you feed them at the right time with an open hand; they eat and are satisfied with the good things you provide. However, when you turn your face away, they tremble with fear because they know their time has come to die – you take away their breath and they return to the dust of the ground.

Your Spirit sustains our planet - new fauna develop – and new flora carpet the ground.

O may the glory of God that we see all around us keep going forever and may God be able to rejoice in all he has made. This God who only has to look at the earth and it quakes, who only has to touch a mountain and it smokes.

I am going to sing to the Lord for the rest of my life, sing praise to my God. May my thoughts and the meditation of my heart always please the Lord, as I find joy in him.

One day, sin will be no more and only those who have been redeemed will be left.

Praise the Lord, O my soul. I will say it again, praise the Lord.

Psalm 105

I am going to praise the Lord, shout out his name, let everyone know what he has done.

I will sing to him, sing praise songs to him, songs that declare all the wonderful things he does.

I will glorify his holy name and express the joy that is in my heart.

I will keep looking up towards his face and gain his strength as I do.

I will remember the wonders God has done, all the miracles and his justice. It is good that all who know him do this.

He is the Lord my God and his justice will one day cover the whole earth.

He is a God who remembers his covenants and the promises he has made forever.

He made a covenant with Abraham which was repeated to Abraham's son Isaac and then confirmed to Isaac's son Jacob, who became known as Israel. This was the everlasting covenant:

"I will give you the land of Canaan as your inheritance."

The covenant was given even though they were few in number and strangers in the land. Even though they wandered from nation to nation, from one kingdom to another.

God allowed no one to oppress them – he even rebuked kings from time to time. "Do not touch my anointed ones," he would say, "do not harm my prophets."

There came a time when one of Jacob's sons, Joseph, was sold as a slave and bought by a wealthy man in Egypt. He was later cast into a prison – his feet bruised by shackles and his neck put in irons. But Joseph was a prophet with the ability to interpret dreams. His interpretations became true and the king of Egypt heard about it, sent for him from prison and released him. He made him ruler over everything he possessed, he had power to instruct princes and teach wisdom to the elders of the kingdom.

When famine hit the region and food supplies dried up, Joseph had made provision and was in place to save the people from starvation. This brought Jacob and his household to Egypt where they later resided as foreigners.

The Lord blessed them and they prospered but became too numerous for the comfort of their host country. The hearts of the king and his household turned against God's people and they were subjugated and became slaves.

God called and sent Moses and his brother Aaron back to Egypt. They performed signs and wonders before the king and in the land.

Darkness covered the land during the day; all waterways were turned into blood, and the fish died; frogs multiplied across the land entering even the bedrooms of the rulers; swarms of flies and gnats filled the air; hail and lightening caused devastation, destroying vines, fig trees and other trees; a plague of locusts and then grasshoppers came without number, eating everything that was green in the land, all the produce from the fields; finally the firstborn of all the Egyptians were struck down.

God brought the people of Israel out of Egypt with all the silver and gold they could carry. No one from their tribes were affected by the plagues.

The people of Egypt heaved a great sigh of relief when they left, for fear had gripped them as to what might happen next.

God provided a cloud covering for his people in the desert by day and a fire to give light at night. He provided quail for meat to eat as well as the manna from heaven. He opened up rocks to provide water that flowed as a river in the desert.

All this, because God remembered his holy promise he gave to his servant Abraham. He brought his people out of Egypt with great rejoicing and dancing and he gave them the promised land, their inheritance, land others had worked for – so that they would become his established people following his precepts and keeping his laws.

Praise the Lord, for he is faithful.

Psalm 106

I will praise the Lord and give thanks to him for he is good to me and his love for me will never end.

No one can tell of all the mighty things God does, or fully declare all the praise due to him.

I know that I am blessed when I am acting justly towards people and doing what is right.

Remember me, Lord, when you are pouring out your mercy; come and save me when you pour out your salvation, so that I can enjoy the prosperity of those you have chosen, share in the joy of your holy nation, receive my kingdom inheritance as I praise you.

I know I have sinned just as my ancestors have sinned, I have done wrong and acted badly.

There was a time when I was in a place where I gave no thought to your salvation plan. Even after my salvation there have been many times I have forgotten your kindness and love; rebelling against you. Yet your salvation is complete and your faithfulness knows no bounds.

You brought me through the waters of baptism, saving me from my adversary the devil, you redeemed me. The baptismal water washed away my sin and drowned the enemy of my soul.

I believed your promises and sang your praises. But how forgetful I can be, forgetting all you do and finding my own plan for my life journey.

In the dry times of faith, I succumbed to temptation and tested the faithfulness of God. Sometimes you allowed me to have my own way but the consequences were never good.

It was easy to become envious of those close to you, but I knew that route would not end well. I knew you are a jealous God, looking for faithfulness in me towards you. I wanted to avoid your discipline. I knew you are a consuming fire, I didn't want to be consumed!

How easy it was to start making other gods, other things to give my time to, other things to idolise. Exchanging you for worthless things.

How easy it was to forget your salvation, the amazing events that led up to that point in my life, the miracles and awesome deeds.

I could understand it if you had abandoned me, even destroyed me, but Jesus stood in the breach, Jesus's blood covered my sin. He had already taken your wrath against me onto himself.

May I take note from your people long ago, who entered the promised land:

May I never despise the good things you provide for me.

May I always believe your promises.

May I never grumble and always obey the Lord, so that your hand will be gentle upon me and it will go well for me.

May I always be faithful to the one and only Lord and refrain from eating the fruit of worthless pursuits.

May my actions please the Lord and blessings flow.

May I stand up for the truth and intervene when it is being ridiculed.

May I never doubt the Lord's provision or his willingness to give me the water of his Holy Spirit.

May I be careful who I befriend and how I get involved in friendship groups, so that I do not adopt ungodly ways or idolise the things some put on pedestals.

May I value my children more than worldly pursuits. May I spare them from being sacrificed on the alters of materialism, money or vain ambition. May I bring them to Jesus instead.

I am sure if I do these things I will remain in the hands of the Lord and victory over the enemy will be assured. I will not be oppressed by demonic activity or subject to their power.

The Lord will be my deliverer as I remain faithful and will thrive in my purity. Should I get distressed, he will hear my cry. He has made a covenant with me which he will never forget and his great love wins the day.

If there is anything that holds me captive, God will make sure I am released. O Lord, save me and gather me with all your people, so that we can give you thanks and glorify your name.

Praise be to the Lord our God, forever and ever. And may all the people say, "Amen!". Praise the Lord.

BOOK 5

Psalm 107

I am going to give thanks to the Lord because he is good and his love lasts forever.

I love telling my story of how God redeemed me from the grip of sin and gathered me, along with countless others from every corner of the globe, into his kingdom.

Some people's stories are incredible. They had been wandering in the desert wastelands of life, rejected and with nowhere to settle. They were hungry and thirsty and their lives were ebbing away, when they cried out to the Lord in their deep trouble. The Lord heard them, delivered them and turned their lives around. He put them on a straight and narrow path leading to an eternal city where they could be citizens forever.

When I see lives that are so touched by God's unfailing love, I give spontaneous thanks to him. I love to hear of his wonderful deeds. I cry with joy when I see him feeding the hungry and satisfying the thirsty.

There are some who ended up in a very dark place, others in prison, because they did evil things and had no time for God. They became bitter towards the world and stumbled around aimlessly with no one to help or care. But somehow, in the midst of their trouble and distress, they cried out to the Lord, who shone his light into the deep darkness of their souls and broke the shackles that bound them.

When I see lives that are so touched by God's unfailing love, I give spontaneous thanks to him. I love to hear of his wonderful deeds. He breaks down the prison gates and cuts through the iron bars to set people free from their captivity to sin.

There are some who did very foolish things and suffered greatly because of their sinful ways. They became so depressed they lost all appetite and no longer wanted to live. But somehow, in the midst of their trouble and distress, they cried out to the Lord, who spoke his life-giving word into their souls. They found healing, their souls revived and they wanted to live again.

When I see lives that are so touched by God's unfailing love, I give spontaneous thanks to him. I love to hear of his wonderful deeds. When lives are so transformed, perfuse thank offerings ascend to heaven and joyful testimony flows from within.

There are some whose lives have been like a ship in the ocean. Awesome and exciting at first, seeing the wonderful works of the Lord at a deep level. But then a severe storm arises causing waves to grow frighteningly high. Like a roller-coaster, their ship rises to the sky and goes down to the depths, causing their courage to melt away. They are no longer steady on their feet but stagger around like drunks in the storm. All faith has drained away and they are full of fear. But somehow, in the midst of their trouble and distress, they cried out to the Lord, who spoke to the storm to be still and the sea to become as calm as a millpond. What peace filled their hearts as he guided them back to a safe place.

When I see lives that are so touched by God's unfailing love, I give spontaneous thanks to him. I love to hear of his wonderful deeds. Let these people use their story to exalt God in the congregation and praise him when the leadership meets.

When people do wicked things the rivers that bring refreshment to their lives will dry up as will the flowing springs and their fruit will waste away.

When God's ancient people arrived in the promised land, God turned the desert into an oasis and the parched land into flowing springs. There was plenty of food as well as the security of the cities.

Fields were sowed, vineyards planted and much fruit was harvested. God blessed them, greatly increased their numbers and their livestock were healthy. But as they began to forget God's ways, their numbers decreased and they found themselves humbled by oppression, troubles and sorrow. Their leaders found themselves wandering again in a trackless wasteland.

But God took compassion on the needy and lifted them out of their affliction and even increased their families like flocks in the fields.

When those who follow God's ways look at this history they rejoice in the righteousness and justice of God. But when those who follow evil paths look, they have nothing to say.

So, if I am wise, I will learn from this and also think deeply about the loving kindness of my Lord.

Psalm 108

A prayer for Wales (UK) – a prayer that can be adapted for any nation. See also Personalized Psalm 57:7-11; 60:5-12

My heart is sticking to you like glue, like good quality glue. I am going to break out in song and compose some music. Come on, soul, wake up and get going! Let's make some loud music early in the morning that will wake everybody up!

I am full of praise to you, O Lord, and I will be singing your praises wherever I go. Your love is so great, it knows no bounds and your faithfulness is sky high.

Be exalted, O God, to the highest place of honour and may all your goodness fill the world.

Save this nation, Lord, help us with your mighty hands; may your church be delivered from its oppression.

I hear God speaking from his throne-room:

"In triumph I will reclaim Abergavenny and bring back the Valleys into my possession. Newport is mine, Swansea is mine; Anglesey is my helmet, Cardiff is my sceptre. Aberystwyth is my washbasin; on Milford Haven I throw my shoes; over Newtown I shout in triumph."

Who will bring us to the fortified strongholds, who will lead us to the Caernarfons?

Is it not you, O Lord, you who seemingly have rejected us and no longer fight for us? O God, we need your help against the enemy, for our human strength is futile. With you Lord, we will certainly gain victory and you will trample underfoot the enemy of the soul of this great nation of Wales.

Psalm 109

My God, as I praise you, please speak to me. The enemy is so deceitful and full of lies. He hates me and attacks without reason. He turns even friends against me, but I will continue to pray, even when I am repaid bad for good. Would you appoint a powerful angel to oppose the enemy, may the accuser become the accused. He will be shown no mercy, his very schemes will condemn him.

May his end soon come and all his demons be destroyed. May there be nothing left of his existence or his evil den. May all his deeds catch up on him and the fruits of his labour be exposed. May evil be a thing of the past and blotted out from the future kingdom of God. May God remember all he has done and cast him and his demons into oblivion.

For there is never a kind thought that ever crosses his mind, but only to hound to death the poor, needy and broken-hearted. He loves to speak curses over people, regions and nations; well, may those curses rebound on him.

The thought of blessing someone is an anathema to him; instead cursing is his stock and trade. May he wear a curse like a coat, like a belt tied around him forever. May this be God's payment to the accuser, to the perpetrator of evil.

O Sovereign Lord, please help me for your kingdom's sake. Out of your loving kindness please deliver me. I am spiritually poor and needy and my heart is wounded. I am fading away like an evening shadow, I am as weak as a kitten. I can hardly stand because I have been fasting, I have lost so much weight and am looking gaunt, much to the delight of my accuser.

Oh Lord, you are my God, so help me and save me because of your unfailing love. Let the devil know that I am in your hand and you are my deliverer. Whilst he curses, may you bless. Whilst he is put to shame, may I rejoice. May he be clothed with disgrace and wrapped in shame.

I will loudly shout out adoration to the Lord and join the congregation of worshippers to praise him, because he stands right next to those in need, to save their lives from the devil who condemns them.

Psalm 110

The Lord says to my Jesus, "Come and sit at my right hand until the day when every enemy will be overcome and lie beneath your feet."

The Lord will extend his mighty sceptre from the Holy City and say, "Rule in the very midst of your enemies."

The troops are ready to do battle for your kingdom cause. They are clothed in the righteousness of their Saviour, and drenched in the Holy Spirit.

The Lord has made a vow that cannot be revoked, "You, Jesus, are a priest forever in the order of the great priest of old – Melchizedek."

The Lord is at your right hand and on the day of battle will crush all your enemies once and for all. All the nations and peoples will be judged on that day and only the redeemed will be saved.

Jesus has drunk deep from the brook of suffering and now can lift his head up, exalted to the highest place.

Psalm 111

I will praise the Lord. I will praise him wholeheartedly amongst leadership groups and in the congregation.

The works of God are awesome and make the people who delight in them really think how glorious and imposing they are. God will do the right things forever, his wonders will always be remembered.

The Lord is full of grace and compassion. He provides food for those who revere him and he never forgets the covenants he makes.

There are times when I have seen his power at work, gaining territory from the devil. God always works faithfully and justly; everything he says can be trusted. His teachings form the very foundations of our world and will never be outdated. They were put in place with all faithfulness and integrity.

He has provided us with redemption through Jesus; his new covenant will last forever. O how holy and awesome is my God!

If we want to walk down the road of wisdom we start by believing in who God really is and then following his directions. Along the way, we will gain understanding of the things that really matter.

Everlasting praise belongs to the Lord.

Psalm 112

I will praise the Lord. There is blessing and happiness when we revere the Lord and delight in following his directions as well as putting into practice his teachings.

Our children will have the right foundations to grow strong and be blessed.

We will prosper and thrive. The right things we do will be a lasting legacy. In the dark times God's light with shine through as we demonstrate grace, compassion and integrity.

When we are generous and have an open hand policy, when everything we do is just and fair, then goodness with follow us.

Nothing will be able to shake us off course and we will be remembered long after we are gone.

Because our hearts are steadfastly set on God and we trust him completely, we have no bad news to fear and nothing to worry about. We find total security in the Lord, what is there to fear? Whatever might come against us – there is victory in the name of Jesus.

When we freely give to those in need, these righteous deeds will be remembered forever. Jesus will one day invite us to take our inheritance, the kingdom prepared for us.

The selfish will see this, but be banished from the kingdom. There will be nothing they can do then, they will realise that they can't take their earthly treasures with them.

Psalm 113

I will praise the Lord. He is my Lord, I am his servant and it is fitting that I praise him. I will praise the Lord both now and forever. It is good to know that the Lord is praised from the moment the sun rises to when it sets in all parts of the world. The Lord is high over all the nations and his glory fills the universe.

There is no one that compares to the Lord my God, to God who is enthroned in glory. I love the way he stoops down to look at the earth, reaches out his hand and raises up the poor and needy from their distress, placing them in privileged places. Or how he sees the tears of the childless woman and answers her prayers.

I will praise the Lord.

Psalm 114

When I was saved from my captivity to sin, from the world's ways, I became a temple for God's Spirit, part of his kingdom.

I entered his kingdom through the waters of baptism, into his promises through the baptism of the Holy Spirit. Faith moved the mountains before me.

His presence causes my world to shake. The rocky places have been made smooth by the springs of living water that flow from within.

Psalm 115

All credit must go to you Lord, any good I do is because of your love and faithfulness.

Some might ask, "Where is your God?" My God is in heaven and he does whatever pleases him. Whereas, so many have senseless idols made by human hands. They may be made from gold or silver, but the mouths they have cannot utter one word, their eyes are blind, their ears deaf and their noses cannot smell a thing. They have hands but they can't feel anything and feet , but they can't move a millimetre. They can't even use their voice box to make a squeak.

Senseless are those who make these idols and those who trust them. I will trust in the Lord, he alone is my helper and defender. He is the helper and defender of all who trust in him.

The Lord never forgets me and always blesses me. He blesses all his people, all who trust and revere him; it doesn't matter whether they are famous or unknown.

May the Lord cause you and any children you may have to thrive. May the maker of the heavens and the earth bless you.

The universe belongs to the Lord but he has given the earth to mankind to look after.

When I am lying in my grave in the silence of the cemetery, I won't be praising God there. It is when I am alive that I will extol the Lord, right now and forever.

I will praise the Lord.

Psalm 116

I love the Lord. A long time ago he heard my voice seeking his mercy and salvation. He turned his ear towards me and so I will continue to talk with him for the rest of my life.

There was a time when death reached out to grab me; a premature grave awaited me. I was greatly distressed and sorrowful. But then, I cried out to the Lord. "Save me!"

Oh, the Lord is so gracious and does just the right things; he is full of compassion. He protects those who are unaware of the dangers surrounding them. When I succumbed to the pressures around me, he saved me.

So now I can find deep rest within, because the Lord has been so good to me. The Lord delivered me from death and dried my tears. He placed my feet on solid ground so that I can spend my life walking with him.

Even in my affliction I was able to trust the Lord, but I was so upset I couldn't trust anyone else.

How can I repay the Lord for all his goodness to me? I can continue to work out my salvation and speak with the Lord regularly. I can keep the promises I have made to the Lord - some of them in the presence of others.

When one of his faithful servants dies, that is a precious moment in the sight of God. I am your servant, Lord; I serve you just as others have done before me. You have freed me from the chains of sin and there is a big thank you in my heart. I will speak out my thanks in praise. I will keep the promises I have made to the Lord – some of them in the presence of others, in the congregation, in your presence.

I will praise the Lord.

Psalm 117

I will praise the Lord, I will extol him. Join me in this, all the nations, all the peoples. Because the Lord's love is so great towards us and his faithfulness will never end.

I will praise the Lord.

Psalm 118

The Lord is to be given thanks at all times, because he is good and his love goes on and on forever.

Let the whole church sing out, "His love goes on and on forever."

Let all the leaders sing out, "His love goes on and on forever."

Let every Christian sing out, "His love goes on and on forever."

When I was between a rock and a hard place, I cried out to the Lord; he took my hand and led me into a wide open space.

The immortal Lord is always with me, therefore I have nothing to fear from mere mortals. The Lord is there by my side, helping me triumph over whatever and whoever is against me. How much better it is to run to the Lord than to trust in human beings? It is better to find security in the Lord than in governments.

When I am surrounded by problems, I declare the powerful name of Jesus over them. There may seem no way out, but I speak out the name of Jesus to make a way. Problems can feel like a swarm of bees attacking me, but when I speak out the name of Jesus against them, they withdraw like an enemy fleeing the battle.

When I was pushed towards the cliff edge and about to fall, the Lord helped me. He is my strength, he is my defender and he is my saviour.

There will always be shouts of joy and victory from the mouths of those who walk closely with God.

He does mighty things. He lifts his hands up high and does mighty things! So, I know I will not die before my time, but live and speak about the mighty things God has done.

I know the Lord disciplines me at times, but this will never lead to my death. I will enter his throne room and give him thanks. Jesus has opened up the way into his presence. I will give him thanks, for he answered my prayers, he has become my saviour.

Jesus became like a stone the builders rejected, but he is now the cornerstone. The Lord has done this and it is truly amazing to me. Day after day I can rejoice and be glad in what the Lord has done.

Lord, save me from those things that get in the way of me being successful for the kingdom's cause.

When I am about my Father's business, I am blessed and am a blessing to others.

The Lord is my God, he made his light shine on me. Now I am able to join all those who are redeemed and bring an offering of exuberant praise into his house.

You are my God and I will praise you; you are my God and I will lift your name high.

The Lord is to be given thanks at all times, because he is good and his love goes on and on forever.

Psalm 119

א Aleph

Happy am I when I do all the right things and walk closely in line with God's ways. Happy am I when I obey God and seek him with all of my heart; I avoid sin when I keep on the straight and narrow path.

Lord, you have laid down foundational and guiding principles of life that I need to fully obey; if only I was more resolute in doing this. When I consider all your commands, I find myself lacking. However, I can still praise you because of the righteousness of Jesus that has become mine. That grace generates a desire to learn more of the way of life you want for me; to be obedient. Your grace means you will never forsake me.

ב Beth

How can young people keep themselves pure? By putting into practice God's teachings.

I will go after God with all my heart. Please Lord, keep me on the straight and narrow. I have endeavoured to absorb your words deep into my heart so that I will not sin against you.

I will praise you, Lord. Teach me your ways. Help me remember and recite your words. I find joy in living according to your guiding principles, there is more joy living this way than in gaining great riches. Your words are worthy of meditation and I love thinking through your path to life. I do consider your ways a delight, so I must not neglect your word.

ג Gimel

Lord, please be good to me all through my life and help me to obey your words. Open my eyes to see the wonderful gems encased in your guiding principles. I am a citizen of heaven and as such a stranger on earth, so let me see clearly your paths for me. Your Holy Spirit has generated a desire within me to constantly follow your guiding principles.

Those who walk their own paths, rather than yours demonstrate an arrogant attitude which will not end well. Some even hold me in contempt because I follow your ways. There are some in high positions in society who speak badly of people like me, people who love to meditate on your word. However, your guiding principles are a delight to me, they have become my counsellors.

ד Daleth

Lord, I am feeling very low, please keep me going by your words.

I talked to you about what was going on in my life and you spoke back. Teach me your ways for my life. Help me understand your guiding principles and think about your wonderful deeds.

I have a weary sadness inside of me, please strengthen me with words from your scriptures.

May all my ways be transparent and full of integrity; would you shower your grace upon me and teach me your ways.

I choose to be faithful to you and have set my heart on keeping your laws. So as I do this, Lord, let me not be put to shame. Now that you have broadened my understanding of your guiding principles, I am able to run in the path of them.

ה He

Teach me, Lord, your principles, because I want to be guided by them to the end of my life's path. Help me understand them so that I will walk in them and obey them wholeheartedly. Keep me walking in the right direction on the right path, because I know that's where I will find true delight.

May my heart turn towards your way of love and not toward selfish gain. Turn my gaze away from what is worthless and keep my life marinated in your word.

May your promises to me be fulfilled, so that I will more fully appreciate that you are God.

As I endeavour to keep your laws, please help others who don't, see that they are good, so that they will not try to shame me. Your Holy

Spirit generates a desire within me to follow your guiding principles and when I am doing that, I get the very best out of life.

ו Waw

May I experience your unfailing love towards me, Lord and the abundant life you promised. Then when anyone taunts me with a question like, 'Why bother with Christianity?', I have the answer, because I trust in your words.

May my mouth be full of the truths found in your word, for this is where my hope lies. It is my intent to always be obedient to you, Lord, for as long as I live. Freedom is found in walking in your ways and that is why I seek out your guiding principles.

I am prepared to speak about your ways to anyone, even kings. I know I will not be ashamed because I delight in your word and love its teachings. I look for the Holy Spirit to guide me in the truths I love, to help me meditate on them.

ז Zayin

The promises in your word bring me hope, even when I am suffering they keep me going.

Those with no regard for you, those with an arrogant attitude, look down on me for trusting and obeying your word. The fact is, I find great comfort remembering your ancient laws.

I do get churned up inside by those who do wicked things to others.

Your words turned into songs, play within me wherever I go. Even in the night, I remember them. They are helpful in keeping me on the straight and narrow.

I always want to make it my practice to follow your guiding principles.

ח Heth

Lord, you are everything I need and I have promised to obey your words. I love the face to face encounters we have and I look forward to your grace flowing over me as you have promised.

There came a time when I reflected on the path I was taking and decided to redirect my steps along your path for my life. How important it is not to procrastinate when it comes to following your guiding principles.

How important it is, not to forget your word when I am surrounded by temptations. Your word is so wonderful there have been times when I have found myself praising you in the middle of the night.

I am happy to befriend anyone who respects you and follows your ways.

O, how your loving kindness can be seen all over the world. Help me understand more about you and your guiding principles.

ט Teth

Lord, may I experience your goodness, just like I read in your word. Would you teach me more about you and your ways, so that I can make sound judgements? I do trust your words.

Your loving discipline has brought me back to following your ways. You are good and all that you do is good. Teach me more about your guiding principles.

There are some who have lied about me out of their own arrogance. But I have endeavoured to follow your ways with all my heart. Their hearts may be hard and unemotional, but I do enjoy studying your word.

Yes, it was good for me to come under your loving discipline, so that I would learn more about your ways. What you have said in your word is more valuable to me than the gold reserves of any country.

י Yodh

You are my maker, you shaped me, so please help me understand and follow your manual for life. May others who love you, rejoice with me, because my hope in your word was justified.

All your ways are right and when I stray from them, you discipline me because of your faithfulness towards me. You have promised me your unfailing love and that is a great comfort to me. May your compassion always flow towards me, so that I may live an abundant life walking in your paths.

There are some who through their arrogance have wronged me without any just reason, but I will continue to dwell on your guiding principles.

May I be someone people can turn to, particularly people who love you and want to follow your ways. May I follow your ways with all my heart, so that I will be a good role model at all times.

כ Kaph

Everything within me longs for you to deliver me from the problems I have right now, but I continue to put my hope in your words. My eyes are straining to see your promises fulfilled, "When will I find your comfort, Lord."

I feel spiritually dry, even shrivelled, but I will not forget your guiding principles. I have to ask how long I have to wait before you deal with those who persecute me? These people disregard your ways and dig holes in which to trap me.

All your words can be fully trusted. Please help me, Lord, for I am being persecuted for no good reason, they have nearly ground me down to dust. But I have kept following your guiding principles. Because of your love that never fails, please keep me going, so that I can continue to be in obedience to all your words.

ל Lamedh

Your word, Lord, will last forever; it is part of the fabric of heaven. Your faithfulness will also endure from one generation to the next for all time, just like the earth that you created. Your laws also have the same longevity and serve your purposes well.

If I had not followed your ways, I am sure I would not be here to tell the tale. I will never forget your guiding principles for they have kept me alive. Deliver me from anything that would get in the way between us, for I belong to you; I have followed your guiding principles.

The devil is like a lion waiting to destroy me, but I am going to keep close to your ways.

Perfection is limited by sin, but your ways know no bounds.

מ Mem

Oh, how I love your word; I like to think about it all the time. Your ways are always guiding me and making me wise. In fact I now have more insight than my teachers of old, more understanding than those who are much older than me, because of my attention to your word and guiding principles.

Obedience to you has been the great aim of my life and has kept my feet from broad paths that lead to sinful ways. You have taught me your narrow path which I have endeavoured to follow.

Yours words are so sweet to taste, even sweeter than honey. I gain so much understanding from your revealed word, so much so, that I hate any wrong path.

נ Nun

Your word is like a powerful torch lighting up my path so that I do not deviate from it. On the day of my baptism, I confirmed my faith in the Lord Jesus Christ and the Holy Spirit placed your laws into my heart.

There have been times when I have been close to death, but you preserved my life as you promised in your word.

Accept my freewill offering of praise and at the same time increase my understanding of your ways. Though my life is in constant danger, I will not let that deter me from following your ways. The devil lays his traps for me, but I have been careful to avoid them by being guided by your principles.

Your words are my rich possession for all time; they bring joy to my heart. Indeed, my heart is determined to keep following your ways to the very end of my life.

ס Samekh

I find people who sway this way and then that in their faith really frustrating. There seems to be a lack of real love for you and your ways. I have made you the place I run to when in trouble; you are my guardian and I have put my hope in the things you have said in your word.

I don't want to spend too much time with those who do evil things, people who could draw me away from following your ways.

Your grace sustains me, Lord – that is what you have promised and my hope is that I will live the abundant life you came to bring.

Keep me strong, Lord and I will get through anything. I will always follow your ways.

Sadly those who reject your way to eternal life will find their broad way will lead them to oblivion. Those who persist in doing evil things will find themselves on the wrong side of God's judgement.

I love your ways, stand in awe of your words and my whole being reveres you.

ע Ayin

Lord, I have tried to do what is right and just; please do not abandon me to those who try to oppress me. I am looking for your favour and protection over my life. It does seem like I have been waiting sometime for you to save me, for your promise to be fulfilled. Lord, I know your unfailing love will prevail.

Lord, teach me your ways, give me a spiritual discernment that helps me understand what you want me to do. Is it not time, Lord, for you to intervene in our world, for your ways are being disregarded.

But I love your ways more than gold bullion, more than 24 carat gold. I know that your path is the right one, which is why I hate all the wrong paths.

꜄ Pe

Your ways are wonderful and that is why I want to follow them. When your words are revealed they light up your ways and give even the most simplest of people understanding.

I am thirsty and long for your words. Would you turn your face towards me and have mercy on me as you always do to those who love you.

Please guide my feet along the path your word marks out and let no sin take me captive. Indeed, let no human being take me spiritually captive either, but let me be free to follow your guiding principles.

May I experience your glorious presence and guide me along the right paths.

When I look around and see people disregarding your ways, it causes a deep sadness in my heart.

צ Tsadhe

Everything you do is right, Lord, and all your words lead me down the right paths. Your guiding principles are always right and totally trustworthy.

I am so passionate about your ways, and what really exhausts me is seeing people following their own ways. I love the testimonies of how your many promises have been fulfilled. I love your promises too.

I may be lowly and in some quarters, despised, but I do not forget your ways. You will always do the right things, both now and forever and all your words are true.

Even when I am troubled and distressed, your words bring me a deep joy. Your ways are always right, please give me a greater understanding of them, so that I may enjoy abundant life.

ק Qoph

So here I am Lord, calling out to you with all my heart. May I hear your answers and I will obey your words.

Here I am, calling out to you. Deliver me from my troubles so that I can continue walking in your ways.

I will get up before the sun rises to cry for your help; my hope is in your words. I stay awake long into the night thinking about your promises.

I know you love me, Lord, and will hear me when I call. I know my life is in your safe hands. The devil may be near devising his wicked schemes that are full of lies, but you are nearer, Lord, devising good plans that are full of truth.

I realised a long time ago that your word is a firm foundation that will last forever.

ר Resh

Lord, would you look down from heaven and see my pain, please take it away, I have not forgotten your words. You have promised abundant life and so I ask that you defend me and rescue me.

For those who keep walking down the broad path to destruction, salvation is far off, they are not looking for your path.

Lord, you are full of compassion for me, thank you for the abundant life Jesus came to bring.

There are many demons that desire my downfall, but I will stick like glue to your words.

My heart is so very sad for those who rebel against you and go their own way.

I love your guiding principles, they help me live the abundant life you so lovingly provided through Jesus.

Every single word you speak is true and your right paths will go on into eternity.

ש Sin and Shin

The Government may try to persecute me because of my beliefs, but my heart will still revere your word. It is like treasure and when you find it there is great rejoicing.

The devil is the father of lies which I hate, but your words are always true, which I love. I will regularly praise you throughout the day as I think about how right and true your word is. There is such peace that flows from loving your word and it prevents me from stumbling along the way.

I long for the time when I will receive your gift of fullness of eternal life, but in the mean time I will keep walking along your path, obeying and loving your wonderful words. I take great encouragement in knowing that all my ways are known to you.

ת Taw

May you hear my cry, O Lord; help me understand what it is you are saying to me. May my prayer reach your throne so that I will receive the deliverance you have promised.

My mouth will overflow with praise like a waterfall as I think about how right and true your words are.

May your hands be there to help me as I am guided by your principles.

I long for the time when I will receive your gift of fullness of eternal life, but in the mean time I will continue to delight in your word. I will praise you as long as I live and your words will keep me fed.

Sometimes I wander away from you like a lost sheep, but you are the good shepherd that comes and finds me, because you know that I have not forgotten you or your ways.

Psalm 120

When I pray and seek God in times of trouble, he answers.

Lord, would you protect my reputation from lies, gossip and deceit. Would you bring your sharp arrows of truth to shoot them down, the fire of your Holy Spirit to consume them?

Sadly there are people living close by who are manipulated by the father of lies, the devil. They do not seem to be remotely interested in peace as I am, but want to stir up trouble all the time.

Psalm 121

I am going to lift my face towards the throne-room of God, for that is where my help comes from. Indeed, my helper is the Lord himself, the one who created heaven and earth.

He will stop my feet from slipping from his path and will watch over me twenty four hours a day, seven days a week, for he never sleeps. O, how comforting it is to know this.

As the Lord watches over me, he provides twenty four hour covering and protection in the heat of battle with the enemy of my soul. The Lord will keep me from all harm; he watches over my life at all times and wherever I am and he will do so right now and forever.

Psalm 122

I was so glad when some friends said to me, "Come and join us in Jerusalem to pray." My feet stood in the gates of the city and walked round the ancient buildings. I came to the very place Abraham and his descendants had come to worship and praise the Lord. The City of David, where Christ will one day return to judge the world.

I pray for peace to come to Jerusalem. I pray for those that love you there to be secure. May there be peace within and without the city walls. May there be peace within the seats of power. For the sake of people across the world, may there be peace within this central city. For the sake of God's church, I pray 'Shalom' over this special city.

Psalm 123

I will keep looking up to the one who is seated on his throne in heaven. In the same way servants would look to their master or mistress for their provision, so I look to you, O God, for the provision of your mercy. Have mercy on me, have mercy on this land I live in. There seems to be no end to the contempt and ridicule of the arrogant and proud, so I pray for your mercy on these as well.

Psalm 124

I am so glad the Lord is on my side and I am on his. There have been many times when he has defended me, rescued me and kept my head above the water. My troubles could have swallowed me up; I could have drowned in them as, like flood water, they swept me off my feet. I could have been swept away and lost forever.

But praise the Lord, he kept me out of harm's way. It is as though I have escaped like a bird from the fowlers trap. The Lord broke open the trap and allowed me to fly free.

I am so glad to say, that my helper is the Lord, the one who made the heaven and the earth.

Psalm 125

Because I put my trust in you Lord, I am like a mountain that is unshakeable and lasts forever. And just like mountains that surround a city, so you Lord surround me, both now and forever.

It is often the case that power falls into the hands of the unscrupulous, but this will not always be the case, for the kingdom of God is coming.

May I be careful not to become unscrupulous myself, but may my heart remain principled, for the Lord does good to those who practice goodness.

However, there will come a time when those who walk on their own broad paths will reach the destination of destruction.

May all God's people know peace.

Psalm 126

When the Lord brought revival to our land, your people's dreams became true. The Spirit brought laughter and new songs of joy into the congregations.

Other nations heard about it and marvelled at what great things the Lord was doing. Indeed, the Lord did do great things and the people were filled with the joy of the Lord.

Would you do it again, Lord. We have sown many tearful prayers into this land and are expectant for a joyous reaping time. You have said that those who go out weeping, carrying the gospel seed to sow, will return with songs of joy as they bring back the harvest of souls.

Psalm 127

I recognise that the Lord needs to be the architect, otherwise I will build my life in vain. Indeed, if the Lord is not watching over my affairs, then any security I may have will be in vain.

My dependency will always be on the Lord, as I trust him he provides. If I trust in my own labours to put food on the table, I may lose peace and sleep.

I thank the Lord for my children, they have been a blessing from him and will continue to be a blessing into my old age. They are like precious arrows in the bow of an archer, ready to defend me when I become vulnerable. I am blessed that my quiver is full. I feel confident that they will support me if I should ever need it.

Psalm 128

I know I am blessed when I revere the Lord and walk according to his ways. I will eat the fruit of my labour and experience blessings and prosperity. I have been blessed with children who have grown up around me and they have children of their own. Yes, how I have been blessed as I have revered the Lord. May all God's people know his blessings showering from heaven and may we all see the church, the body of Christ, thrive throughout our lifetime.

I thank God that I have lived to see my children's children.

May there be peace in Israel.

Psalm 129

The church has been persecuted from its birth on the day of Pentecost two thousand years ago. In its early days there was great persecution, but it came through victorious. The backs of your people were ripped by whips and lion's claws.

But the Lord always does what is right and out of this wicked oppression arose a stronger church.

The church still suffers great persecution in various parts of the world. May the persecutors realise how shameful this is and turn from their wicked ways. May they wither away like crops without roots in rocky soil, may their numbers diminish so they become ineffective. May it be clear, that God blesses his people but not their oppressors.

Psalm 130

From deep within my soul there is a cry to you, O Lord, would you turn your ear towards me, hear my voice, listen to my cry for mercy. I am so glad that, because of your love, you keep no record of wrongs, if you did, no one could stand before you. But you are a forgiving God and your grace inspires me to serve you.

I wait for you Lord, my whole being waits for you. I wait for your words to reach me and give me hope. I wait for you, with a longing greater than a night security guard waits for the morning.

My hope is in the Lord, he is unfailing love personified and I have full redemption through Jesus Christ. Indeed, it was God himself that took on the form of a man and came into this world to redeem me from all my sin.

Psalm 131

I endeavour not to harbour pride in my heart or look down on anyone. I only want to focus on the works you have prepared for me and not concern myself with matters too weighty for me or way beyond my understanding.

I have found peace through simply following your ways and trusting in you like a child trusts its mother. There is contentment living like this.

So, I am going to put my hope in the Lord right now and always.

Psalm 132

Lord, would you bear in mind all the sacrifices I have made for your kingdom's cause? I have been intent to see your presence once again reside in this land. Sometimes this desire has led to periods away from home and prayer meetings long into the night.

Prayer has been heard in centres across this land. People have gathered from the four corners of the land to pray for your Spirit to once again fall on this land, for you to make a dwelling place here. Arise Lord, we prayed, may your presence come.

May your church leaders be full of integrity and intent on doing the right things. May your faithful people overflow with joy.

You promised long ago to King David that one of his descendants would be the Messiah, the anointed one, who would be seated on his throne. He would be King of kings to reign forever and his name is Jesus.

The Lord chose Jerusalem long ago as his final dwelling place where he would reign on his throne forever. It is his intent to bless this city, satisfy the hungry and bring the religious leaders in-line with his ways. His faithful people will overflow with joy forever.

It is here that the Lord will establish Jesus as King and he will truly be the light of the world. A radiant crown will be placed on his head and all his enemies will know their final destiny.

Psalm 133

It is so good and a real pleasure to see God's people in relational unity. It is a work of the Holy Spirit that starts with leadership and then finds its way into and across denominations and congregations.

When this happens it prepares the ground for a harvest of souls, for the Lord imparts his blessing of new life, the sort of life that goes on forever.

Psalm 134

I will praise the Lord, especially when I meet with others to pray through the night in God's house. I will lift my hands high in worship and praise. O may I know God's blessing showering upon me, the blessing of the Creator of the universe.

Psalm 135

I will praise the Lord. I will praise his name along with my brothers and sisters in Christ, with those who come to the house of God or wherever we worship.

I will praise the Lord for he is good, I find singing praise to him such a pleasant thing to do.

I know that the Lord has chosen me to be his child, to be his treasured possession. He is great, beyond comparison to any other god. The Lord is able to do whatever pleases him, whether that is in heaven or on earth or in the depths of the oceans.

He is able to make clouds form and send lightening with the rain. From his atmospheric storehouses he brings out the winds.

He intervenes for the cause of his people, sending signs and wonders and bringing down obstacles along the way. Throughout the course of history, God has been at work amongst the nations and its kings for his redemptive purposes.

It will be the Lord's name that will last forever; the Lord will be known through every generation. In the end his people will triumph; he will have compassion on them.

How lifeless are the man-made idols people worship. They may be fashioned from precious metal, but their mouths cannot utter a word, their eyes are completely blind and their ears have no hearing. Those who make them and those who trust them will also become lifeless one day.

As for me, I will trust and praise the Lord. Come on, all God's people, all who revere him, let's praise his name together. Praise be to the

Lord who dwells in every heart that bows the knee to Jesus. Praise the Lord.

Psalm 136

I am going to thank the Lord, for he is so good. His love is endless.

I am going to thank the God of all gods. Yes his love is endless.

I am going to thank the Lord of lords for his love is endless.

Only God can do such great wonders. His love is endless.

With his infinite wisdom he made the heavens. His love is endless.

By his command the earth formed out of the waters. O his love is endless.

He made the stars and planets. His love is endless.

There is the sun to light up the day. His love is endless.

There are the moon and stars to bring light into the night. His love is endless.

He provided his firstborn as a sacrifice. O yes, his love is endless.

He brought me out of slavery to sin. Let me tell you, his love is endless.

With his mighty power he defeated death. Let me remind you, his love is endless.

He brought me through the waters of baptism. His love is endless.

And swept away the enemy of my soul. I have to tell you, his love is endless.

He has led me through my spiritual journey. His love is endless.

He has brought down giants that threatened me. His love is endless, yes it really is.

They became like grasshoppers before me. His love is endless.

This obstacle, flattened. His love is endless.

That obstacle, removed. His love is endless.

So that more of his kingdom could come. His love is endless.

And eventually I will receive an eternal inheritance. I have to say it again, his love is endless.

He found me when I was lost. His love is endless.

And freed me from the enemies power. O his love is endless.

He is my provider. Yes, his love is endless.

So, I will give thanks to my heavenly Father, for his love is endless, yes his love is endless, I will say it one more time, his love is endless.

Psalm 137

In the mountains and hills of Wales I sat down and wept when I remembered the times of spiritual revival in this land. With a heavy heart I put down my musical instruments. How could I play songs of joy when the enemy of my soul taunted me with the state of the church; tormenting me with words like, "These lyrics aren't relevant anymore." "How can I sing the songs of revival in such a wayward society?"

But I can't forget the church in those days when it flourished, it would be like forgetting who I am. If I forget, then I might as well never sing again. The church is the body of Christ and it is his highest joy and mine.

Remember, Lord, how the enemy brought the revival to an end. "Let the church never flourish again," was his cry, "May the very foundations be destroyed."

There is coming a day when the devil is doomed to destruction and all his demons will be cast into the fiery pit with him.

Psalm 138

Lord, I am going to praise you with everything within me. You come before anything else and I will sing your praises. I will kneel before you and praise you for your love that is endless and your faithfulness towards me. You have kept your promises to me which has brought you into sharp focus in my life.

You were there when I called out to you, you answered and gave me much courage.

How wonderful it will be when all the world leaders praise you, which they surely will when they understand your words and redemptive plan. They will sing about the ways of the Lord and how great you are.

Even though you are so great, Lord, you look with kind eyes on the humble, unlike the arrogant who are not even in your line of view.

I may walk through difficult times, but there you are walking with me, taking care of me. You demonstrate your power against the enemy of my soul and save me from his schemes.

Your enduring love and amazing grace will sustain me to the end of my life's purpose, you will never forsake me.

Psalm 139

Lord, you are able to see through the exterior of my life - you know me inside out. You even know what I am doing at any time and what I am thinking. Nothing is hidden from you and nothing is a surprise to you - you even know what I am going to say before I speak! You know me better than I know myself.

Having you in my life is like having my own personal bodyguard. How wonderful it is to think that you, the Lord of the universe, have your hand on my life - it just blows my mind.

And there is nowhere I can go without you being right there with me. If I climb to the top of Mount Everest, or journey to depths of the Indian Ocean in a submarine - you will be there with me. Whatever time zone I am in, whatever distant country far from home, you will be right there with me, guiding me and upholding me.

When darkness is all around me and even within me, I am not hidden from you. You are light personified, you shine brightly into that darkness like a powerful search-light - darkness is nothing to you.

You are the one who created me to be who I am; like a potter, you shaped me in my mother's womb just as you wanted me to be. When I think about this vessel you have produced, how intricate and wonderful it is - I just want to praise you. In fact, all that you do is truly amazing. To think that even when I was forming in the womb, you were there by your Spirit, your watchful eye was supervising the process. You filled in my life's calendar before I was born.

How incredible your thought processes are, O God; how infinitely great the number of them. They are as uncountable as the grains of sand at the beach. And you are with me 24/7 - how precious is that!

I do have a problem with evil people - why don't you get rid of them? They speak bad things about you and misuse your name. I find myself hating those who hate you. Your enemies have become my enemies.

However, I want to ask you to take a look deep down inside me, do some heart searching and mind mapping. Are there things that I am doing that you don't like; anxious thoughts that have no place? If you find some - lead me away from such things so that I can enjoy the abundant life you have for me.

Psalm 140

Lord, I know the devil is like a roaring lion, looking for those he can devour, so please protect me and when necessary, rescue me from his claws. His evil schemes stir up conflict all the time. He causes people's words to become poisonous, their tongues as sharp as a razor. So, keep me safe from such things, Lord, protect me, so that I don't trip up. The devil is a master at setting hidden snares, dark nets and traps along my path to entangle me.

But I will keep thinking about you Lord, you are my God and will hear my cry for mercy. You are sovereign, my strong deliverer and will shield my mind which is such a battleground.

Will you send angels to thwart demonic activity, may the devil's plans be unsuccessful. I know there are more angels surrounding me than demons in the heat of battle. May the ugly spiritually dark forces find their lies backfire.

One day, the devil and his cohorts will find themselves thrown into a fiery pit from which there will be no escape. May those who slander others and those prone to violence experience the justice they deserve.

It is good to know, Lord, that you will secure justice for those in poverty and will stand up for the cause of those in need. I for one, will praise you and love the free access I have into your presence through the sacrifice of Jesus.

Psalm 141

Lord, here I am again, calling out to you. Please answer quickly, may I sense your presence. May my prayer rise up to your throne as I lift up my hands towards heaven.

Lord, my tongue always has the potential to poison someone, so please help me to tame it, keep a watch over what words my lips may form. Lead me not into temptation, but deliver me from evil. Put a guard on my passions and do not let me eat the attractive fruit that will lead me away from you.

May I find those who I can be accountable to, who will speak into my life and rebuke me if needed. It is wise for me to surround myself with godly advisors as I pray against the deeds of darkness.

There will come a time when evil will no longer triumph and those who do evil things will realise the error of their ways.

Sometimes a situation seems hopeless, but my eyes are not fixed on the problem but to the one who is sovereign over all. It is in you, Lord, that I find refuge and strength to overcome anything.

Keep me safe from the devil's traps, from the snares he lays before me. May his demons fall into them as I avoid them all together.

Psalm 142

Lord, I am crying out aloud to you, the inner petition for mercy has found a voice. It is all pouring out to you now, my problems and troubles. My inner strength is fading away, but I know you keep watch over my life.

As I walk along my life's path, there are the devil's snares hidden to trap me. Right now, it feels like there is no-one walking alongside me, no-one concerned about me, no-where in which I can take refuge and no-one who cares.

So, here I am Lord, crying out to you. You are my refuge; out of all who live on the planet, you are the one I can truly count on.

So, please listen to my desperate cry for help and rescue me from the demons who pursue me, they are too strong for me to fight off on my own.

I feel imprisoned by my current circumstances, but if you set me free, I will be able to praise you. Then others who love you will see the goodness you have shown me and rejoice with me.

Psalm 143

Lord, please hear my prayer, listen to my cry for your intervention. You are so faithful and always do the right thing, so please show me your mercy rather than judgement. I stand before you clothed in the righteousness of Jesus.

The enemy is in hot pursuit, trying to crush my life into the ground, drawing me into a dark place where I feel I may as well be dead. My spirit is but a faint whisper of what it usually is and my heart is downcast.

I am going to think back to days when I have seen you at work. Ponder on the wonderful things you have done. Spread out my hands before you. I am thirsty for you Lord, like someone in the heat of the day longs for water.

I need a quick answer, Lord, because my spirit is hanging by a thread. Please don't hide your face from me, if you do, I will feel like death warmed up.

When I wake up in the morning, may there be good news of your love that never fails me. I am trusting in you, Lord; I have put my whole life in your hands and I need you to show me the way I should go.

You are the one who delivers me from the enemy as I hide myself under your huge wings.

Lord, teach me your ways, for you are my God. May your Holy Spirit guide me along level ground for my feet. Lord, you are always true to who you are and do what is right, so please keep me safe and deliver me out of my troubles. Out of your unfailing love for me, your servant, silence the enemy of my soul and destroy his dark forces.

Psalm 144

I am going to praise the Lord. He is my Rock, he trains me up for spiritual battles so I can stand firm. He loves me and is my castle, my safe place. He delivers me from trouble and shields me from the fiery darts of the devil. I can truly find refuge in him as he fights my battles.

I sometimes wonder why you care for human beings, us mortals – why you even think about us. After all, we are just like a breath that appears on a cold day and then disappears. Our days are like a fleeting shadow – visible for a while and then a cloud covers the sun and it is gone. And yet you do care and you do think about us.

So, would you part the heavens, Lord, and descend to earth. Touch the mountains of difficulty in my life so that my troubles burn away. May lightening scatter the enemy of my soul; shoot your ammunition and rout him.

Would you reach down from heaven with your mighty hand and deliver me from the devil's grip; his mouth is full of lies and his ways are deceitful. Rescue me from the rising flood waters of trouble.

I am going to sing a new song to you Lord, from deep down in my spirit. I will sing about the victories and deliverances you bring.

I know you will deliver me from the deadly weapons of the enemy of my soul, whose mouth is full of lies and his ways so deceitful.

I look forward to the time when the youth in the congregation are thriving like well-nurtured plants, becoming pillars of society. When the church will be filled with every kind of provision and the congregation will multiply. When the fruit of our labours will generate a great harvest. When the spiritual walls of the city will no longer be breached by the enemy – no longer will he take people captive and no longer will there be distress in our streets.

Oh, how blessed we will be when this happens and how blessed are we now, because God is our Lord.

Psalm 145

I am going to lift you up in praise, my Lord and King; I am going to worship you forever into eternity.

Every day I will praise you and exalt you now and for eternity.

For the Lord is great; no-one can get anywhere near measuring his greatness and he is so worthy of all praise.

From one generation to the next, your works have been praised; the mighty things you do have been recounted; the glorious splendour of your majesty has been sung about. It is good for me to think about your wonderful works.

I want to talk about the power of your awesome works; shout from the roof tops your great deeds. Your abundant goodness together with all the right things you do are surely things to celebrate with joyfully songs.

O Lord, you are full of grace and compassion, you don't get angry quickly and you are so rich in love. You demonstrate your goodness to everyone and your compassion to all the things you have made.

All the things you have made shout out your praise, as do all those who are faithful to you. I love to speak about your glorious kingdom and mighty power, so that more people know about the wonderful things you do and the glorious splendour of your kingdom. Your kingdom will last forever and you will reign through all generations.

Lord, all the promises you make are trustworthy and you are faithful in all you do. You stoop down from heaven and lift up those who have slipped or who are burdened with a heavy load.

In your wisdom you designed a world that sustains all living things; it is as if the eyes of all look to you and you give them food at just the right time. How marvellous this is. You open your hand and the desires of all living things are satisfied.

You always do what is right and you are always faithful to what you have said. I love the way you are near to me when I call, how amazing that this is the case for all who call on you with integrity.

You delight is fulfilling the desires of those who revere you; your ear catches their cry and you rescue them. You watch over all who love you, however, sadly there are those who go their own way, which will not end well.

Lord, my mouth is full of praise to you. May every creature on earth and in heaven praise your holy name both now and forever.

Psalm 146

I will praise you Lord. Out of the depths of my soul, I will praise you. I will praise you every day and sing your praises for the rest of my life.

It is pointless putting my trust in human beings, even people of great stature, because they cannot save my soul or know what is round the corner. When we die and return to dust the earthly plans we had come to nothing.

How blessed I am when I trust you Lord to help me, when my hope is in you, the Lord of lords and the King of kings. You are the maker of everything in heaven and earth and sea. You have always been faithful and always will be.

The cause of those oppressed is your cause too. You provide food to the hungry, proper justice for the prisoner and sight to those who are blind. You reach down from heaven and lift up those who are stooped over with heavy burdens. You love it when people do the right thing. You hate racism and keep watch over those who suffer from it and you have a special place in your heart for those bereaved of a father or husband. On the other hand, you frustrate the plans of those who do evil things.

You, Lord, will reign forever, through all generations and beyond. O how I want to praise you.

Psalm 147

I will praise the Lord, O how good it is to sing songs of praise to him. There is something very pleasant about praising God and it is certainly a fitting thing to do.

It is the Lord who builds his church and gathers the lost into his fold. He heals those whose hearts have been broken and attends to their emotional wounds.

The Lord is so great, that he controls the number of stars in space and gives each of them a name. The Lord is so great, his power so awesome and his wisdom and knowledge so limitless.

The Lord lifts up the humble, but humbles those who do evil things.

I will gratefully sing praise to the Lord with a melody composed by the Spirit.

The Lord created the ecosystem that works so well: the clouds that supply rain to the earth which makes the grass grow, which in turn provides food for cattle. The Lord provides food for all, even the pesty young ravens who call out.

However, the Lord's real pleasure is not in the magnificent strength of a horse, or even the strength and agility of a warrior, but he takes delight when I revere him and put my hope in his unfailing love.

So, come on church, lets praise the Lord. Let's look to him to help us stand against the devil's schemes, to bless us, to bring peace and unity and a great harvest of souls.

The Lord still sustains the universe with his words: he commands the snow to cover the ground like wool and the frost like ashes; down comes the hail like pebbles. No-one can survive for long in sub-zero temperatures without adequate protection. And then, he speaks again and the snow and ice melt in the south winds – the streams and rivers resume their flow.

I am so grateful that the Lord has revealed his word to me, his ways and guiding principles for my life. Being a child of God is certainly a privileged position like no other.

I will praise the Lord.

Psalm 148

It is time to praise the Lord!

Let praise resound from heaven, from the lofty heights above; all those angels, all the heavenly host – praise him! But not just angelic beings, let all the things God has made shout out praise to him for being as awesome as they are: the sun, the moon, the shining stars too many to count – the whole universe and the atmosphere around the earth. Let these things praise the Lord, for he commanded and they were created and not only that, but they have been established with physical laws for all time.

Let praise resound from earth, from the deep sea to the highest sky: the creatures that live in the oceans and the meteorological manifestations such as lightening, hail, snow, clouds, stormy winds – let them praise the Lord.

O and there are the magnificent mountains and rolling hills, the fruit trees and all the trees of the forests, the wild animals and the cattle, the small creatures and the flying birds, together with kings and queens, presidents and rulers, young men and women, old people and children – let them all praise the Lord, only he is worthy of exaltation, his splendour and majesty is universal.

Through Christ, God's faithful people, those close to his heart, have power and authority to do exploits which bring praise to the Lord.

It really is time to praise the Lord.

Psalm 149

I will praise the Lord. Sing new songs composed by the Holy Spirit in the gatherings of God's faithful people.

Let the whole church sing joyful songs to their Redeemer King, let us rejoice because of all he has done and all he is. Let us praise him with spontaneous dancing and make music before him inspired by the Spirit. For the Lord delights in us and our humility before him; he will adorn us with an eternal crown.

What an amazing honour – something to truly rejoice about – in fact when we think about this at night in our beds, we may find a song of joy bursting out!

May praise for the Lord be found in my mouth and the double-edged sword of his word in my hands. With these two things, I will be able to inflict damage to the devil and his forces of darkness and bind and loose things in spiritual realms.

What an honour for God's faithful people to carry out his purposes.

I will praise the Lord.

Psalm 150

I will praise the Lord. May all God's people praise him, may all the heavenly hosts praise him – both earthly temples and heavenly palaces united in praise.

Let's praise him for his acts of power. Let's praise him for his greatness that surpasses everything.

Let's praise him with the saxophone, praise him with the harp, praise him with the guitar, praise him with the tambourine and dancing, praise him with the violin and keyboard, praise him with the drums and a loud clash of cymbals.

Let everything that has breath praise the Lord!

I will praise the Lord.

.

Printed in Great Britain
by Amazon

84721786R00129